W9-CKE-852

Essentials for Chaplains

Edited by
Sharon E. Cheston
and
Robert J. Wicks

Paulist Press

New York/Mahwah

Copyright © 1993 by Sharon E. Cheston and Robert J. Wicks

All rights reserved. No part of this book may be reproduced or transmitted in any form or by any means, electronic or mechanical, including photocopying, recording or by any information storage and retrieval system without permission in writing from the Publisher.

Library of Congress Cataloging-in-Publication Data

Essentials for chaplains/Edited by Sharon E. Cheston and Robert J. Wicks.
   p. cm.
Includes bibliographical references.
ISBN 0-8091-3420-9 (paper)
1. Chaplains. 2. Clergy—Office. 3. Pastoral theology.
I. Cheston, Sharon E. II. Wicks, Robert J.
BV4375.E77 1993
253—dc20
                        93-26013
                            CIP

Published by Paulist Press
997 Macarthur Boulevard
Mahwah, New Jersey 07430

Printed and bound in the
United States of America

Contents

A Brief Introduction v
       Sharon E. Cheston, Ed.D. and
       Robert J. Wicks, Psy.D.

1. "Burnout" 1
       Robert J. Wicks, Psy.D.

2. Sexual Abuse of Children 9
       Sharon E. Cheston, Ed.D.

3. Dealing with Anger 24
       Duane F. Reinert, O.F.M. Cap., Ph.D.

4. Facing the Faces of Grief 34
       Anthony F. Krisak, S.S., S.T.D.

5. Guilt and Shame 48
       William J. Sneck, S.J., Ph.D.

6. Working with the "Chronologically-Gifted"   60
       Edward R. Killackey, M.M., M.S.

7. Dealing with Confrontation 73
       Anthony J. DeConciliis, C.S.C., D.Min.,
             Ph.D.

8. Anxiety: A Personal Discernment 91
       Ann O'Shea

9. Crisis Intervention 101
       Beverly Elaine Eanes, R.N., Ph.D.

10. When the Patient Is a Woman 110
       Anne Ross Stewart, M.R.E., M.Div., D.Min.

Notes on the Contributors 139

Dedication

In Memory of
Sister Helen Hayes, O.S.F.

A Warm, Professional and Distinguished
Pioneer
in Pastoral Health Care

A Brief Introduction

The development of a book for chaplains entitled *Essentials for Chaplains* was an idea proposed at the initial meeting of the NACC Education Task Force. It was felt that a monograph containing essential pastoral care information on an array of current topics was needed. Given the very demanding schedules of today's chaplains, the goal was to provide succinct practical material on key topics as well as suggested readings for those wishing a more extensive treatment of the subject in question.

The areas decided upon were: "burnout", sexual abuse of children, anger, grief, guilt and shame, "the chronologically-gifted," confrontation, anxiety, crisis intervention, and women's issues. In each case, a special effort was made to select an author who was familiar with both the topic area and the unique demands of modern chaplaincy.

Essentials for Chaplains was also written not only to provide practical information on certain topics but also in the hope that it would serve as a model for future monographs. The idea was that if this material proved helpful, other issues could be covered in similar ways under the editorship of others in the membership of the NACC so an ongoing exchange of clinical pastoral expertise would continue. For our part here, we are grateful to have had a role in providing assistance through this work to those persons so intimately involved with the spiritual and emotional well-being of the physically ill and their families: today's pastoral health care professionals.

Sharon E. Cheston
and
Robert J. Wicks

Graduate Programs in Pastoral Counseling
Loyola College in Maryland

1

"Burnout"

Robert J. Wicks, Psy.D.

∾

To many chaplains, the danger of what is referred to in the literature as "burnout" is a daily reality. The ability to reach out to patients, their families, and medical staff members without being pulled down themselves in the process must at times seem to chaplains like "pure grace." The nature and quantity of pastoral care demands in contemporary health settings are so overwhelming and complex that to even begin to formulate a strategy for chaplains for emotional and spiritual survival seems futile.

Part of the reason for this is that many problems facing those ministering in health care facilities are in fact unsolvable at this point. In addition, since the role of the chaplain—notwithstanding the existence of a job description—is in reality often quite open-ended, there seems to be no natural boundaries to the expectations of patients, their families, and the institution's staff. Being "another Christ" is a dangerous image to have in the eyes of persons with extreme needs and sometimes unanswerable questions—i.e. "Why is my little boy dying? He's only eight years old and he's been so good and brave for a little boy his age."

However, despite these difficult realities, there are very clear and helpful psychological and spiritual points worth remembering which can often prevent unnecessary stress from arising or unavoidable pressures from taking an inordinate toll. To be helpful though, they must be repeatedly read, reflected upon and prayed about individually and with colleagues and friends; otherwise their message will not take root.

If we do not "overlearn" the lessons of stress reduction for the care-giver, we risk building our pastoral care ministry on sand—a very precarious step given the storms of anxiety, depression, and stress that committed chaplains must encounter today—and every day! The point being made is: The situation is not going to get better in today's pressure-filled health care settings, and a one-time workshop fix or literature review on stress won't do. (How many times have all of us gone to a conference on stress or read a book on it, only to put the suggestions aside within the next few days?) Only a deep honest reliance on God and actively seeking healthy psychological and spiritual perspective through a continual review of essential keystones on burnout prevention will help. So, it is in this spirit that the following ten things to remember on "burnout" are offered.

∾

1. Solitude and Silence

Practically every person in ministry can wax eloquently on the value of following the call of Jesus to his followers to go off by themselves to be absorbed in prayer (Mk 1:35). However, the sad reality is that more people than imaginable attempt to undertake intense ministry without a time set aside each day for prayer in silence and solitude. There are many reasons for this, but two classic ones are that (a) quiet time to be with God is quite awkward and "unfriendly" to many people and (b) God is not seen as important or as relevant as action on behalf of others is (especially in the case of care of the sick and their families). However, unless this time is taken our self-esteem, purpose, and compassion will all lose their fervor in time. Given this, two ways to overcome the resistances noted above to prayer are as follows:

(a) Set out a time in the morning which is enjoyable for prayer. In other words, with your morning coffee, tea or juice sit down for only five minutes and just relax in silence and solitude with God. Don't worry about doing anything, don't fret over distractions, just be there with God as a good friend. Since it is only five minutes (staying longer of course is good), never vary from it even if you are busy and it will become part—the central part—of your day.

(b) Be reflective during the day by occasionally imaging yourself in the presence of God. Real spirituality dawns when God becomes as real as the problems and joys we face each day. And one way for our life in the spirit to become more of a reality is to live our day reflectively.

2. Detachment

Urban Holmes, an Episcopal seminary dean, once noted: "The opposite of detachment is not compassion —it is seduction." By that he meant that we are seduced by others' unrealistic expectations and the crazy expectations we have about ourselves rather than being concerned about what God is asking of us. The questions people ask chaplains are in many instances unanswerable. In fact they know it when they ask such things as: "Why is God allowing me to be sick so much of my adult life?" The important role for the chaplain is to be detached enough from the persons in their suffering to be clear and strong enough to stand with them in their pain. All of us cross the boundary occasionally; this is a natural danger of compassion and care. However, the point to remember is *not* to try to carry the crosses only meant for *God* so our arms can be free enough to carry the crosses *we* are expected to bear.

3. Ongoing Education

Reading, conversations with other professionals, and conferences are excellent ways to reignite the excitement and commitment we felt when we entered the field originally. With respect to ongoing professional reading, the following is suggested: As well as reading short passages each week from sacred scripture, the choice of one work in psychology, one in theology, and several in spirituality to read and focus on each year is a suggested minimum.

4. Friendship

Given the hours and type of work pastoral care professionals do, it is sometimes difficult to have the time to interact with friends. However, after prayer, this is one of the most important areas to attend to as a way of preventing burnout. In addition to having healthy friends to visit and relate with who tease, inspire, challenge, support us and help us laugh at ourselves, we should seek to have friends we can write to and call on a regular basis to round out our support group.

5. Physical Health

When our physical health is good, we can withstand more stress than when we are not healthy. Sleep, regular meals, and exercise are essential. To overcome the temptation of ignoring the need to attend to these areas (which of course is easy to do), I try to get into a regular pattern of rising and going to bed, eat light meals often (so I don't feel deprived and turn to "junk food"), and don't set ridiculous exercise goals for myself that I will never meet and thus about which I will feel guilty! Instead, I try to take a walk each day—on two or three days the walk being a long one.

6. Leisure

Time off is often seen as selfish and unnecessary. This is a particularly "North American" attitude. Other cultures seem to recognize the need for leisure. I have a very busy schedule but I always take time each day for mini-coffee breaks, and I enjoy hours of quiet time wherever I can get them. Since I see leisure as valuable to my having the energy to be truly available to others if they are in need, I plan quiet times during the day and week and usually get them. I think that so many of us are tied to the image of being a "busy, overworked care-giver" that whether we admit it or not, we have difficulty giving up this image. And there is some validity to this; after all, if we are honest we can see that people who seem rested and at peace often draw the ire of those who are not. But having said this, being overwhelmed and unrested is still too high a price to pay for the so-called "advantages" of having such an image.

7. Balance

Each of us has a unique balance in terms of such poles as: stimulation and quiet, reflection and action, work and leisure, self-care and the care of others, self-improvement and unfolding patience, future aspirations and present positive realities, and involvement and detachment. We must find the balance that best suits us. For some of us more quiet time is necessary; for others, stimulation is a must. Therefore, in the former case, time alone is a necessity, whereas, in the latter case, leisure time with others after work is needed. Since balance is so unique to each person, time for reflection on these areas and discussion with friends or a spiritual director would be a good idea.

8. Effectively Dealing with Negativity

There is a real need to be aware of the negative thinking we often have about ourselves when things go wrong or we have unpleasant interactions with others. Correcting one's cognitive errors so there is a greater recognition when we are exaggerating or personalizing situations in an inappropriate, negative way is essential if we are to survive in a milieu which is often filled with depression, sarcasm, despair, and futility. In addition, being able to communicate our own angry feelings in an effective way is also essential. Unexpressed anger, as is mentioned elsewhere in this book, can be like a psychological cancer within our personality. Techniques in recognizing and expressing anger allow us to confront situations in a way that helps us experience a sense of self-respect and power even in those situations which are unpleasant and, for the time being, unchangeable.

9. Self-Appreciation

We need to reflect on what gifts God has given to us each day and to be grateful for them. By doing this we set the stage for solid self-esteem and a sensitivity to ourselves which enables us to best nurture and share our talents with others. To really appreciate ourselves we must have some reasonable level of self-awareness. Anything that can increase such a level (discussions with friends, reflective reading of books on psychology and spirituality, spiritual direction and counseling, etc.) is recommended.

10. Use Multiple Levels of Success

Unlike in other areas of medicine, pastoral care's impact—no matter how behavioral we get as a result of current movements in that direction of health care administration—is often intangible and difficult to measure. Moreover, even in those areas that are measurable, we may not be able to see the impact we have had. For instance, in standing with a family of a person who has been critically injured in an automobile accident by a driver who was impaired because of alcohol abuse, there may be a great deal of negativity expressed in the chaplain's presence. After the encounter the chaplain may feel used and abused and see nothing positive in the interaction, only to find out later how much it meant to the family that he or she stood with them during this difficult time. By using multiple measures of success we take the time each day to see the many things we have done which may have had an impact; this then offsets some of the seemingly negative results of the day's efforts.

ᠭᡅᢣᡉ

The above list is obviously not exhaustive. In reviewing it and by possibly reading some of the material suggested in the following list, my hope is that the reader will make up a unique list for himself or herself with an eye on the particular spiritual and psychological "weak spots" he or she has.

Self-knowledge can lead to self-help or self-condemnation. The goal of this chapter on burnout has been to have chaplains become more self-aware so that such gentle self-help is undertaken because a chaplain with a heart full of love and peace always has much to share.

Suggested Readings

Edelwhich J. and Brodsky, A. (1980). *Burnout: Stages of Disillusionment in the Helping Professions.* New York: Human Sciences Press.

Gill, J. (1980). "Burnout: A Growing Threat in the Ministry," *Human Development,* 1 (2), Summer, 21–27.

Wicks, R. (1992). *Touching the Holy: Ordinariness, Self-Esteem & Friendship.* Notre Dame: Ave Maria Press. (See especially chapters on self-esteem and friendship.)

——— (1991). *Seeking Perspective.* Mahwah, NJ: Paulist Press. (Please note chapter on "Reaching Out Without Being Pulled Down.")

——— (1990). *Self-Ministry Through Self-Understanding.* Chicago: Loyola University Press. (See especially chapter on "Burnout and Commitment.")

2

Sexual Abuse of Children

Sharon E. Cheston, Ed.D.

ᗡᕦ

Sexual child abuse is one of the greatest horrors of our society. When these tragic events are reported or exposed, chaplains are often the helpers on the front line of highly intense interactions involving the victim, the abuser, the family, friends and other staff. Because of the emotional reactions involving the accusation of sexual abuse, many will want to deny, under-react, over-react or blame. In fact, no occurrence raises our moral conscience or heightens our instinct to protect and punish the way that sexual abuse of a child does.

Perhaps the most devastating problem that exists in cases of child sexual abuse is that the abuse is usually perpetrated by a trusted friend or family member. Sexual molestation or abuse by a feared stranger is a rare occurrence. Therefore, when sexual abuse occurs the child and family not only have the sexual abuse and all its ramifications to deal with, but also the issue of trust destruction. This last issue permeates the child's view of the world, can have long-lasting effects and is one of the major concerns that a chaplain will have to address.

It is difficult to understand the personality flaw that would cause an adult to violate a child's physical boundaries to the extent of sexual abuse. There are many theories as to how this happens. The most prevalent of these include:

- Children are at the bottom of the power ladder and are treated as property or as less then fully human and therefore not entitled to the same respect as adults.

- Our society is a sex negative society in which sex is utilized to sell products and therefore leaves the impression in many people's minds that sex is an area to be exploited.

- Some adults have poor boundary definition causing them to see others as not being differentiated humans with feelings.

- Some people equate sex with love and affection and are convinced that sexual involvement with children is the appropriate way to show children love and affection.

Chaplains interact with all those who are a part of the sexual abuse: the victim, the abuser, the victim's support system, other possible victims and the staff ministering to all those listed above. Below are ten items to keep in mind when you, as chaplain, work with children who have been sexually abused and their significant others.

∽

1. Get Involved But Remain Calm

When the secret of sexual abuse is revealed, there are several different reactions those involved may have.

There are tendencies to deny the abuse, become angry, indulge in blaming, become hysterical, or withdraw and leave the problems for others to solve. Chaplains provide a very special service at the time of revelation and subsequent interactions. Therefore, their posture needs to be availability, interaction and calm presence. Listening is always one of the most useful tools for chaplains and is particularly important during the revelation stage of sexual abuse. Everyone involved has a story to tell and intense emotions are felt. Strong emotions evoke strong emotional reactions; therefore if the chaplain experiences the desire to withdraw, feeling that the situation is best handled by clinical personnel, then he or she needs to acknowledge that this feeling is normal but also unjustified. While the clinical personnel will be closely involved with the psychotherapeutic aspects, the chaplain can be the person who provides the calm ear and a sense of trust. In tandem the chaplain provides the family with a God representative. Questions emerge such as: "Why does God allow this to happen? What is evil? Should we be passing judgment or is that God's job? What do I do with my hatred? Is it a sin to hate the abuser and wish him or her dead?" Obviously there are no answers to these penetrating questions of pain, and often the persons involved are not looking for the answer, but they need to ask the questions out loud to someone who will not judge them for asking the tough questions. If the chaplain avoids the situation or puts on a clinical hat, then the questions may be asked in silence and never expressed. The involved chaplain can provide the impetus to expression. The chaplain's calmness will encourage uninhibited expression of emotion from everyone involved. One note of importance—the chaplain needs to take this same stance with the helping staff too. Helpers and hospital staff can be traumatized by the work that they have to do and will need to debrief. Chaplains who reach out and stay open to listening can assist with catharsis in the middle of the horrific charges and investigation.

Remaining engaged and yet calm will also be of help to the children who have been abused. These victimized children feel like pariahs. While in some cases the families are supportive of the child, there are many cases where the family blames the child for causing the ruckus and disrupting the homeostasis of the family system. The children, though correct in speaking up, feel like outcasts and may begin to wish they had not spoken. The chaplain's job is to establish a trusting relationship that is supportive of the child. This takes patience and time, especially if the chaplain is the same sex as that of the abuser. The energy devoted is well worth the effort even if it does not appear to be so at first. Years later, victims report that they were hanging on to their sanity through the one person who was not blaming, questioning, challenging or degrading them.

2. The Child Needs To Be Supported Even If the Accusation Is Not Immediately and Easily Confirmed

The question as to whether to believe a child who is making an accusation of abuse has been debated for over one hundred years. Even Freud uncovered sexual abuse, including incest, and believed the reports of the victims, only to buckle under the weight of public and professional outcry. He then recanted and chose the position that these victims were fantasizing about being abused.

Thus was born generations of psychotherapists who denied that sexual abuse was as prevalent as was being reported by their patients.

At the very least, a child who reports sexual abuse needs not to be disbelieved. While the double negative may seem to be unnecessary, there is a difference in stating that the child needs to be believed and the child must not be disbelieved. The outcome is that the chaplain can be open to the child, non-judgmental and supportive. This position will allow the child to talk more freely, and thus the chaplain will be in a better position to gather more information to enhance the entire intervention team's effectiveness.

The greatest hesitancy to believing the child's report seems to stem from the fear that an innocent adult will be accused and that the repercussions from the false accusation will be devastating. While there is no argument that a false accusation is terrible, so is the effect of sexual abuse on a child. Also one must remember that, for a child, the act of revealing abuse is fraught with much danger. Usually the child has been threatened with death, harm, or rejection if he or she reveals the sexual abuse. In addition, the child is told that he or she will lose family and friends. If a child is able to overcome these terrifying threats and seek help, then the child deserves to have someone listen. Also, experts report that the younger the child, the more likely the child is to be telling the truth. An older child could be seeking revenge or attention by accusing an innocent person, but careful listening, noting inconsistencies in statements, as well as physical examination will often reveal the deception. Therefore, if you are unsure of whether to believe the child or not, then supporting the child without supporting the accusations can be a safe position for the chaplain.

3. Sexual Abuse of Children Creates Many Victims

Whenever sexual abuse is made known, helpers and authorities focus immediately on both the victim who revealed the information and the victimizer. In the scurry not only to stop the perpetrator from carrying out the threats, but to stop the sexual abuse, and to obtain the medical help needed, the system may forget that there are others who may have fallen victim to the tragedy. As the chaplain, you may have occasion to be ministering to the family, too. The spouse in particular will need special attention during the discovery. He or she may or may not have known about the abuse, but either way he or she will know that the ramifications of such a revelation will cause the family to be scrutinized if not destroyed. Life as the family knows it will cease to exist. The spouse may even feel apprehensive, expecting that he or she will be held responsible for not protecting the child from the abuse. Likewise, the older siblings may feel guilty if they have been victims themselves and did not reveal the abuse, thus allowing it to happen to the younger sibling(s). These family members will need special ministering, for the guilt can become cancerous or may turn to anger against the victim for upsetting the homeostasis of the system. The logic would seem to be that if they kept their mouths shut and survived the abuse, then the victim could have also.

Younger siblings could also have been victimized and may need the chaplain to be available in case they feel strong enough to come forward. This cannot be rushed even if there is suspicion that the abuser sexually abused the other siblings. Children will reveal only what they believe it is safe to reveal. Listen and watch the younger siblings carefully: they will frequently divulge their wish to talk through non-verbal behavior.

Grandparents and other family members can be quite helpful to the family, or they can be a great distraction or even an impediment. The latter will be particularly true if the abuse has been ongoing throughout the generations. The chaplain will be of inordinate help with these victims because they will be the most neglected by others who are involved in helping the family.

4. Legal Issues Vary from State to State

Each state has a law concerning the protection of children from sexual abuse. All state laws have mandatory reporting of any suspected child abuse, particularly sexual abuse. Included in the law is a release from liability for those who make a good-faith reporting of abuse. Chaplains who are ordained ministers may feel that they are exempt from the legal reporting of abuse because of the long-held precept of separation of church and state. However, most states still require ordained ministers, chaplains, pastoral counselors and vowed religious to report suspected child abuse if it is discovered during counseling, hospital visits or any other non-confessional setting. Some states have upheld that the confessional act is exempt from this reporting mandate. However, the person wishing to make a confession is the one who determines the confession. In other words, a confession becomes a confession when the person says "I wish to make a confession" or something similar. The priest or confessor cannot talk with a person, hear of an abusive situation, and then decide that he or she will invoke the seal of confession. Therefore, unless a chaplain is hearing a confession that has been identified up front as such by the confessor, he or she must report any suspected child abuse to the proper legal authorities. Since each state has slightly different reporting procedures and time frames, it behooves chaplains to know the laws of the states wherein they serve.

Further, the chaplain's job is not to conduct the investigation. The chaplain need only report the suspected abuse. Let the legal investigators investigate. Once the investigation takes place the responsible agency will recommend the disposition of the perpetrator and the family, including the victim. Once again, laws vary, so it is important for chaplains to know the laws of their respective states. This knowledge will be helpful since, during the revelation period of sexual abuse, one of the major concerns of the family, the victim and the perpetrator is the legal ramifications. In fact, this fear can consume those involved, overshadowing the concern for the victim.

5. Your Feelings Are Normal

All helpers are faced with hearing difficult patient stories and observing terrifying circumstances. What one chaplain handles with the greatest of ease, the next chaplain cannot handle at all. However, sexual abuse tends to arouse intense emotional reactions from all of us. Acknowledging that these feelings are normal is a first step to being able to deal further with the perpetrator, victim and family. Talking with other helpers who are involved with the case will garner support and allow catharsis. Remember to take care of yourself.

Overwhelmed: Traditionally these types of situations overwhelm the most experienced mental health worker, chaplain and state worker. If you find yourself overwhelmed, your colleagues probably feel the same way.

Angry: It is easy to become angry when faced with incidents of sexual abuse. The perpetrator can draw our rage, the victim can cause us to be angry when refusing to cooperate, the family can enrage us when it denies or blames. Anger can be deleterious to working with families but it does not need to be. Properly channeled anger can energize and make chaplains more determined to provide appropriate help.

Victimized: Dysfunctional families tend not only to scapegoat their members but also to victimize or scapegoat the helpers who are trying to bring about healing. This feeling of being victimized can provide clues as to how the family functions and thus help the chaplain to avoid the victimization or help him or her to aid others who also feel the sting of victimization. This will especially surface if the chaplain is the person who must report the abuse.

Fearful: Because of the seriousness of sexual abuse and because sexual abuse can be linked to the perpetration of violence, the chaplain can feel fear of the perpetrator and/or other family members. If a chaplain fears for his or her safety, then it is prudent to take the necessary precautions to assure everyone's security.

6. Use the Correct Words

Human sexual body parts and sexual acts have much euphemistic language connected with them. In fact there is so much euphemistic language that we often forget that we are speaking in euphemisms. Sexual abuse situations mandate the use of correct, appropriate words when describing the body parts and the sexual acts. While children do not have this vocabulary, it is important for chaplains to use the correct words for clarity. For example, one five year old girl told me that she hurt when her grandfather touched her "bee bee." I had no idea what a "bee bee" was, so I asked her to point to it. She pointed to her rectum. I asked her if there was another word that described that part of her body and she said, "Yes, my bottom." I accepted that word to be closer to the real word and used the word "bottom" when talking with her, although we were still using a euphemistic expression. When speaking with others who are involved, the use of appropriate, correct words clarifies the nature of the abusive acts.

7. Sexual Abuse Permeates the Entire Person: Physical, Intellectual, Emotional, Social and Spiritual

Children who are sexually abused must be treated on all levels. Obviously the child's physical health and safety will be the first concern, and there will be many helpers to assist in this area. The emotional component needs to be addressed by mental health professionals, though it is important for chaplains to be aware of the child's emotional states during the conversations. Abused children tend to be intellectually distracted. Because of poor concentration, they are forgetful and clumsy. Some professionals even connect accident proneness to the child's distractibility. Socially and developmentally, abused children tend to be more advanced for their age in their knowledge of sexuality and may even appear quite mature. However, the child is usually quite emotionally insecure and immature, having skipped developmental stages by being forced into sexual acts at a very young age.

Spirituality is the chaplain's primary area of expertise, and the child will have many tough questions if you are open to them. The child may be enraged at God for having let this horrible thing happen. On the other hand, the child may feel that God is the only "person" who cared and has gotten him or her through the terrible moments. One young girl prayed to God to take her away from the experience and then as if by magic she would have an out-of-body experience in which she flew up to clouds and stayed there until the abuse was over. Although she was angry at God for letting her father abuse her, she realized later that God had indeed answered her prayers by allowing her to dissociate.

Another spiritual reaction can be alienation from God. The response is a logical one: "If God does not care about me, then I do not care about God." As the chaplain you represent God to the child, and if the child senses your care for him or her, then this will go a long way to rebuilding the idea that God does care. This is also true when the child feels unworthy in the eyes of God because of the abuse. The chaplain's unconditional love and acceptance for the child demonstrates the belief that the child is a worthwhile human being and a child of God's.

Most sexual abuse (90%) is perpetrated by an adult male on a young girl. The spiritual transference that occurs in many female children is that male authority figures use their power to hurt; since God is the ultimate male authority figure, therefore, "God will hurt me too." Each time the abuse occurs, this idea is reinforced. In this manner, the female child becomes more and more afraid of God. Therefore, the child may act afraid of male chaplains. Knowing this, the chaplain should arrange for a female chaplain to see any young girls who have been abused by a father figure. The basic rule of thumb is that, at first, the child should be seen by a chaplain of the opposite sex from the perpetrator.

8. Intervention Is Necessary for Change To Occur

When sexual abuse is brought out into the open, the perpetrator and the family may try to convince all the helpers that the abuse will stop immediately. There may be pleas and promises to this effect in order to avoid any further disclosure or involvement with authorities. The chaplain should keep in mind that change will not occur without intervention. Systems are very resistant to change, and in order to impact a system, confrontation is needed and follow-up to assigned activities is essential.

In addition to the systemic issues, the victim needs support and protection from retaliation and the abuser needs to be held accountable for the seriousness of the abuse.

9. The Child Is the First Concern

When a child suffers abuse and it is made known, the adults involved, particularly the perpetrator, will usually be louder and more verbal than the child. This activity can detract from the child's safety, which is first and foremost the major concern. The child needs to be the central focus. He or she needs to have physical security and a safe person to talk to who takes the position that what happened is wrong and is in no way the child's fault. The parents may be blaming the child for blowing the whistle rather than looking at the child as someone who needs protection and love. All intervention should take the child's needs into consideration first or the child can be forgotten.

10. The Abuser Is Totally Responsible for the Abuse

It is not at all unusual for the perpetrator and for other family members to attempt to diffuse the blame for the sexual abuse away from the perpetrator and involve others. Some systems advocates have unwittingly done this by always insisting that the spouse is somewhat responsible and had to know about the abuse on some level, and further, that if the spouse did not do something to stop the abuse, then the spouse is culpable too. This spreading of the responsibility to others includes, sadly enough, the victim. One abuser told anyone who would listen that his nine year old daughter was very seductive and wanted him to have sex with her, so he was doing so at her request. I must admit the child did look seductive for her age and had much more sexual knowledge and experience than any nine year old should have, but the fact remained that this façade was probably an outcome of the sexual abuse and not the cause of it. Even if the child was seductive prematurely and this facade was not due to sexual abuse, still 100% of the responsibility for maintaining boundaries rests with the adult. The uneven balance of power means that the adult must always say "no" to impulses and desires. In the same vein, while others in the family may not have recognized the covert or even overt signs that something was wrong; no one else in the family is responsible for the sexual abuse except the victimizer (Rencken, 1989).

It is only through this stance that those involved will begin to crystallize what has to happen in order for the perpetrator and the family to move toward health.

First the perpetrator must see the action as an error in judgment and own it. Next the child victim must be told by the perpetrator that the child is in no way responsible for the abuse. An apology from the abuser with a promise that it will never happen again is also an important part of the healing process. This apology needs to be made in front of the other family members and all helpers.

∽

Sexual abuse of a child is one of the most horrific experiences that a child can suffer. Chaplains will have the opportunity to interact not only with the victim but frequently with other family members and the perpetrator. Because of the unique role that a chaplain plays, the family members involved will receive support and an open ear to their pain. A chaplain's work makes a major contribution at a time when trust has ebbed and betrayal is a by-word. The chaplain can assist all involved to deal with the tragedy, set boundaries, face the pain, allow catharsis and thus instill hope.

Suggested Readings

Bass, E. and Davis, L. (1988). *The Courage To Heal*. New York: Harper & Row.

Butler, S. (1985). *Company of Silence*. San Francisco: Volcano Press.

Finkelhor, D. (1979). *Sexually Victimized Children*. New York: Free Press.

Finklehor, D. (1984). *Child Sexual Abuse.* New York: Free Press.

Lew, M. (1990). *Victims No Longer.* New York: Harper & Row.

Rencken, Robert H. (1989). *Intervention Strategies for Sexual Abuse.* Alexandria: AACD.

Rush, F. (1980). *The Best Kept Secret, Sexual Abuse of Children.* New York: McGraw-Hill.

Russell, D.E. (1980). *The Secret Trauma.* New York: Basic Books.

3

Dealing with Anger

Duane F. Reinert, O.F.M. Cap., Ph.D.

ᢙ

"Chaplain, would you stop by Room 1252 and see Mary? She's really angry today. Thanks."

Requests of this kind can make chaplains cringe. Dealing with an angry person can indeed be a challenge. Most of us do not have an innate comfort level when interacting with angry people. Yet we know that it is important to acknowledge anger and deal with it when we encounter it. Running away from anger is neither pastoral nor constructive.

If a chaplain learns that the anger is not directed toward him personally, it is much easier to tolerate. Therefore, for the chaplain's own comfort level, quickly determining the object toward which the anger is directed can be fruitful. Ambiguous situations produce anxiety in most of us, so clarifying what we are dealing with can have a calming effect.

The chaplain can also learn certain skills which are helpful in dealing with an angry person. With some training and experience, it is possible to become more comfortable and effective in dealing with anger (Sharkin, 1989).

Anger is not the same as aggression or hostility. Anger is an internal, autonomic response. In contrast, aggression is an overt, behavioral, and destructive response (Berkowitz, 1972). Hostility can be described as the negative feelings that persist indefinitely after anger

24

subsides, even with no apparent ongoing cause to fuel it. Examples of hostility are resentments, grudges, and long-standing desires for revenge. Alschuler and Alschuler comment that "anger is a situational, temporary response with distinct autonomic components and facial expressions" (1984, p. 26). They note that anger may increase the chances of aggression and hostility but that they are not always caused by anger, nor are they inevitable consequences of anger.

Although humanity has dealt with anger from the beginning of time, the collective wisdom of the ages still has not provided all the definitive answers. We continue to learn to deal with anger in more constructive ways. The following pages offer some practical suggestions for chaplains to remember when dealing with anger.

∽

1. Remain Calm

The first thing for a chaplain to remember when dealing with an angry person is to try to remain calm. Often called into situations without being thoroughly briefed, the chaplain finds such calls anxiety-provoking in themselves. If the chaplain arrives to meet an angry patient, the anxiety level can be quite high indeed! Whether the occasion is a crisis, an emergency, or simply a routine pastoral visit, the chaplain strives to maintain a calm emotional stance in order to accurately assess the circumstance and to react intelligently, effectively, and pastorally.

The chaplain can be most effective with an angry patient by presenting a peaceful, calm persona. In general, an angry person responds to the emotional climate in which he finds himself. If the chaplain is uneasy, the additional anxiety may fuel the patient's agitation. If the chaplain projects a controlled and confident air, the tone he sets is likely to defuse a potentially volatile situation.

2. Assess the Situation

In dealing with an angry person, one would be advised to assess the degree of anger, the situation which provoked the anger, and the person or object toward which the anger is directed. The degree of anger can be conceptualized as being on a continuum from mild irritation on the one extreme, to rage on the other. The chaplain will want to consider the degree of anger in order to choose an effective strategy in dealing with the patient. An enraged patient can be unpredictable and may be easily provoked by the otherwise innocent remarks or behaviors of others. Some specific things to consider when dealing with an enraged person are noted below.

The chaplain will also want to assess the circumstances which precipitated the anger and the object to whom the anger is directed. This information provides clues for the formation of an effective response.

3. The Angry Person Is Not Your Enemy

The angry person is not your enemy; he or she is probably just a person who is experiencing a lot of pain. Anger is normal and is generally a response to feeling hurt. Most of us learn early in life to not enjoy being in the company of an angry person. Our early experience of a parent getting angry at us, scolding us, yelling at us, and similar distasteful events planted the seeds for our later consistent negative response to those who are angry. For those who have experienced abuse in their personal history, an angry person may even be perceived as a danger or a threat.

Given our negative feelings about anger, it is an easy step not only to dislike the emotion itself, but also to evaluate the angry person negatively. The chaplain may need to consider making a decision to reinterpret the situation. The chaplain could reframe it by asking, "I wonder what is causing this person such pain that he or she is responding so angrily?" It is possible that this angry person feels that he or she has been treated unfairly or even abandoned by a family member, by the doctors, or by God.

Anger can be a way of putting some protective distance between the harsh realities of life and one's emotional vulnerabilities. Interpreting anger as a sign of hurt puts the chaplain "on the patient's side" rather than in an adversarial or a defensive stance. The chaplain responds with tenderness and sensitivity to those who are hurting.

4. Look for Subtle Signs

Besides the overt and obvious content of communication, covert messages filled with anger can be communicated through the patient's tone of voice, body posture, gestures, and facial expressions. With some training and experience, the chaplain can become more attuned to the veiled signs of anger.

We have all seen the forced smile that hides a volatile issue, or the hollow ring of someone parroting a religious dogma of hope when anger at God over a tragic loss is just below the surface. In these instances, if the chaplain acknowledges that anger is perfectly understandable and communicates a willingness to listen, the flood gates will likely open and the anger will gush forth. The ability to recognize and correctly interpret non-verbal signs, especially when the anger is escalating, can be a very valuable skill for the chaplain.

5. Anger Can Be Constructive or Destructive

Anger, and one's response to it, can be constructive or destructive. The emotion of anger can be caused by such things as physical discomfort, the frustration of goal-directed activity, and injured self-esteem (Alschuler and Alschuler, 1989). When anger is in response to physical discomfort, it can be constructive because it signals a need to respond to a physical problem. Relaxation or some form of tension-reducing activity can be a constructive response to this form of anger.

Anger may arise when some goal-directed activity is frustrated. For example, when a person offers an idea in a group and no one seems to react or pay attention, it can produce an angry response. The anger which arises in response may signal a need for learning more assertive behavior. In this example, the person could not only present the idea but also request feedback from the group in a more direct manner, while still treating other group members respectfully. In this case, learning more assertive behavior could help reduce anger-provoking situations in the future.

Anger may signal hurt feelings or injured self-esteem. When anger flows from this cause, it is important for the chaplain to reassure the person of his or her value and worth. The simple act of taking time to listen carefully to the angry person makes all the difference in the world. The attentiveness communicates: "You are so valuable to me that I will spend the time and energy necessary to hear your point of view."

If we tune in to our own emotional responses, it will come as no shock that many times our anger flows from our distorted thoughts and interpretations. It seems quite human to impute motives to behaviors which we observe. When we are the one who has been hurt by another, we usually do not give that person the benefit of the doubt—we generally impute condemnable motives. Our distortions fertilize the growth of our righteous anger. If we would make the effort to calmly request that the other describe his or her motives, we might be surprised at the absence of venom directed our way.

The chaplain's long-range goal might be to help the patient recognize the distortions that he or she has imposed on reality. Arriving at this goal is often easier said than done. Obviously, arguing with the patient about the misconceptions or otherwise directly attacking the distortions will probably be perceived by the patient as a threat or a hostile act. However, teaching more assertive behavior to the patient could help reduce anger-provoking situations in the future.

6. Do Not Play with Rage

When anger escalates to rage, the chaplain should remember the basics. The first is safety. Remember, the enraged person is not thinking logically or acting rationally; someone should be attending to the safety of all concerned. If others are present, such as other staff members, but not enough to guarantee safety, someone should be instructed to call for assistance.

The chaplain, and anyone else present, should attempt to maintain an air of calm and control. Softly but firmly spoken words can be more effective than loud and agitated commands. Often very soft conversation spoken in a reassuring vein can defuse a tense situation.

Attempting to discuss the topic which enraged the person will likely fuel the rage. Therefore, it is worth trying to direct the patient's attention to some other topic to allow the physical and emotional arousal to diffuse. If the patient reacts negatively to the diversionary topic, the chaplain may need to abandon it in favor of another.

Non-verbal behaviors of the chaplain or staff also send messages to an enraged person. Moving toward the person, gestures directed at the person (e.g. pointing), staring, and the like can be perceived as threatening, inflammatory, or even attacking. It is important to be sensitive to the multiple ways behavior can be interpreted.

Common sense dictates that one must be attuned to how the enraged person is reacting to the surroundings and the attempts of the chaplain or staff to restore calm. Some techniques work with some persons. There is no substitute for calmly thinking on one's feet!

7. A Little Empathy Goes a Long Way

Empathy, combined with the use of basic helping skills, is probably the most effective approach for dealing with an angry person. Empathy has an "as if" quality. We try to see the world "as if" we were looking at it from the viewpoint of the patient.

Empathy does not mean agreeing with the person or taking the person's side in a conflict. It does not mean having the same feelings that the person has. It does mean that one develops an appreciation, an understanding, of where the person is coming from. It involves being able to see things from a perspective which is similar to the patient's.

If we have some degree of empathy, we can "see" why the person is angry. We can "see" why the situation was so painful to the person. We may even have some clues concerning the distortions in the person's thoughts and judgments. From an empathetic position, the chaplain can respond to the person in a manner that communicates care and understanding—but not necessarily agreement.

8. Beware of Pat Answers

Suppose an angry person pours out complaints to a chaplain. While listening, an answer to the problem becomes very obvious. The chaplain proceeds to offer advice and to provide a solution, only to be summarily dismissed by the patient who, by the way, is still just as angry as before. What happened?

Perhaps the person did not sense that the chaplain was "truly cognizant of his or her pain and being treated as a problem to be solved rather than a person to be understood. Perhaps.

Be cautious of a "one cure fits all" or a "cookbook" approach to people. Human behavior is complex. Like an iceberg, some aspects are known and seem clear to us, but much, much more lies shrouded in the depths of mystery.

It has been popularly held that suppressed anger causes physical problems, that catharsis is necessary to "get it out of your system," that aggressive expressions of anger get rid of it (Tavris, 1989). It is now recognized that talking about anger or expressing anger aggressively to try to get rid of it may actually make some people more angry than they were previously. A more effective solution for some may be not to express anger or talk about it, but rather to engage in relaxation or meditation techniques, jogging, or "catching" themselves getting angry and then redirecting their thoughts to an entirely different topic.

9. Do Not Discount Your Influence

Remember that you have influence and power simply from your position as chaplain. Do not discount that fact. For some people, being in the presence of the chaplain has a calming and soothing effect.

Chaplains occasionally wonder what they have to offer in certain situations—especially if they are not particularly expert in psychology or crisis intervention. On the other side of that coin, a patient may attribute a great deal of power and influence to the chaplain since this is the one who represents God. Some may interpret this as a placebo effect; others may see the grace of God at work. No matter what the perspective, the chaplain can draw on a sense of mystery and use that in the service of the patient.

10. Let God Be God

Some people get angry with God or religion when they feel they have been treated unfairly—for example, when they have been diagnosed with cancer, lost a relative or friend in death, lost a job, and so on. In anger, the person will likely say things that are rash and not well-considered. It may be particularly painful for a chaplain to hear his or her faith attacked so gratuitously and vehemently. Some sobering questions may prevent the chaplain from responding in unproductive anger: Does God really need a chaplain to defend religion or God? Can God withstand this person's attack or will God somehow be diminished if I don't intervene?

The chaplain's role in this instance may be to communicate by his or her physical presence that God is present, accepting, and not vindictive. Later, when the anger has lifted and a clearer head prevails, the belief that God truly loves and accepts unconditionally will likely have a much deeper meaning for this formerly angry person. The chaplain will have fulfilled his or her mission.

∾

Suggested Readings

Alschuler, C.F. and Alschuler, A.S. (1984). "Developing Healthy Responses to Anger: The Counselor's Role," *Journal of Counseling and Development*, 63, 26–29.

Berkowitz, L. (1972). *Aggression: A Social Psychology Analysis* (Vol. 6). New York: Academic Press.

Sharkin, B.S. (1989). "How Counselor Trainees Respond to Client Anger: A Review," *Journal of Counseling and Development*, 67, 561–564.

Tavris, C. (1989). *Anger: The Misunderstood Emotion* (rev. ed.). New York: Simon & Schuster, Inc. (originally published in 1982).

4

Facing the Faces of Grief

Anthony F. Krisak, S.S., S.T.D.

ᕦ

She stands darkened amidst a grove of yews in the center of Rock Creek Cemetery in Washington, D.C. She compels and she frightens, she lures and she admonishes, she weeps and she stares, she excites and she stills. She is the sculpture "Grief." In the presence of this stark figure, both grief and death at once, people waken to the complexity and soften before the simplicity of the destiny we share. In the presence of this aged and ever-youthful statue, memories and wonders of past and future are aroused.

When grief takes on a human face and an audible, passionate voice, it becomes all the more piercing and painful, all the more evocative and holy. This human encounter with the cries and hopes of grief presses the chaplain to a new level of self-awareness, as human limit wrestles with faithful promise. With those chaplains who will walk this holy ground of encountering grief and, doubtless, be moved to manifold memory, ten things to remember are humbly proposed.

ᕦ

1. Grief Wears Many Faces

Strongest among the sources of grief lies death, whether as prospect on the part of a terminally ill patient or as loss among family and friends. The face of this grief over death is multiple, as death may arrive after a long illness or with the unexpectedness of a tragic mishap. Few wear well the face of grief at a time of death, and none can be expected to grieve with decorum. All such grief commands compassion, presence and respect, for in its presence the chaplain meets a vulnerable and breaking heart, no matter what the incidental circumstances may be.

With families of one who has died, the chaplain's encounter with the face of grief will be a short one in which the chaplain sets a stage for the family's transition to the funeral rites and to living in the face of loss. With doctors and hospital staff, the encounter with forms of grief will be ongoing and will be one way in which hospital personnel can wear down the hard shell which often develops in the face of constant loss and pain. With patients experiencing grief in the face of impending death, the encounter will be more elastic and provide opportunity to walk through a variety of "stages." In the case of neonatal death or the death of a child, chaplains will encounter the most intense face of grief where words have little meaning and where the loss contradicts the life-giving purpose which once created a deep sense of joy.

Yet the face of grief waits not only for death but is met at any time of loss. The loss of a limb or its use brings on the grief of imperfection. The loss of ability to carry out the most basic bodily functions stands behind the grief of powerlessness. The loss of speech or hearing creates a barrier with treasured others and engenders the grief of isolation. The seeming loss of faith in front of myriad hurts seeks expression in the grief of meaninglessness. All such grief commands compassion, presence and respect, for the heart lies open in its wounded fragile state, no matter what the source.

Logic may defy some grief, but its presence and intensity will remain for the bearer. Sometimes the chaplain just may not understand why a person's grief is so deep or so intense. Chaplains who are aware of their own limitedness will not allow a lack of understanding to minimize their respect for the unique grief of each person. These chaplains will realize that the face of grief carries a logic of its own to which the cerebral alone is inadequate for reply.

2. Making Eye Contact with the Faces Counts

Surprise touched me when a mother gently chided her young daughter for not maintaining eye contact as we were introduced to each other. That young girl was in the process of learning how directness (with the eyes) in communication is crucial for a genuine human encounter. Likewise, chaplains learn that in the basic response to grief, there can be no ducking. Both literally and figuratively, the eye contact which chaplains establish with the faces of grief is vital. Chaplains acknowledge, verbally or non-verbally, that they hear the pain, and their demeanor betrays that they are not afraid to be with the broken or the weeping. In other words, it is key for chaplains to face grief honestly and head-on.

Lack of "eye contact" with grief is revealed in platitudes which try to smooth the pain or in conversation which tries to sidetrack the grief to brighter and/or cheerier paths.[1] Lack of eye contact reverts to claims of understanding what the grieving ones are experiencing and recounts the people who have been through similar situations. Lack of eye contact supports a cultural tendency to avoid the pain: "Get well soon" (so that we can re-establish contact in a space with no rough edges). In responding to families in an emergency room who have been stricken by unexpected grief, lack of eye contact means offering ways to get over the crisis instead of responding to the cry of hopelessness in an exclamation like "How will we be able to live without him/her!"

Genuine eye contact with the faces of grief invites deepened expression of the grief, and does not wince or glance away when that expression is unanticipated or unfamiliar. Genuine eye contact with grief may even share the sadness and cry with, thus enabling the patient to recognize how acceptable and natural the grief is. Genuine eye contact, with its respecting empathy, sends a subtle counter-cultural message: in your loss, I see you as a whole and dignified person.

The shades of eye coloring must also be acknowledged. The greens and blues and browns and grays of the eyes which face grief are the horizons of faith and hope as well as the diverse cultural traditions which comprise the experience of the person facing loss. In the encounter with grief, chaplains meet people of diverse denominations and faith traditions. They meet people of cultures different than their own.

This means that chaplains are aware of their own responses and ways of handling grief so that they don't unconsciously project their modes of expressions on others. It further means that chaplains are ready to learn various religious and cultural ways of dealing with grief and death or approaching death.[2]

3. Each Person Bears a Unique Time and Rhythm

Popularization of the "stages of dying" has aided all of us in identifying the elements of a life process and in drawing upon inner resources for coping with the various ways in which grief finds expression. Where popularization has become dangerous is where the stages of dying have been interpreted as categories or descriptions into which the grieving must fit or where the process has been understood as a prescription for appropriate grief when it is experienced in the correct order.

My limited experience testifies that hardly anyone experiences the process of grief exactly as it is described in textbooks and handbooks. Anger, disbelief, denial, bargaining, resignation, acceptance, may be voiced loud and clear. But the voice and the timing is as unique as each individual whom the chaplain encounters.

Consequently, chaplains can't push the process of grief, but they can walk compassionately with those who are going through the process. What is important with terminally ill persons is not that they experience every stage of what is described as the grief process but that they be able to appropriate what they are experiencing. Very practically, for example, it can be easy for a chaplain to glance over someone's denial of death by expressing the hope that he or she will soon find acceptance (often voiced in prayer). Respect for the uniqueness of the individual entails listening to and responding to the expressed denial and even making the denial a part of any prayer which the chaplain and patient may share.

In respecting the individual in grief, chaplains assure that the encounter in the midst of grief will remain personal. Such encounters can slip away from the personal and into the "general" if chaplains take comfort in citing statistical information or in making observations about human nature (e.g. "how natural it is for people to feel anger or surprise"). Often the motive for such observations is to assure those who grieve that they are not alone. Chaplains, however, who recognize the personal nature of their encounter also recognize that the primary way to send a compassionate message is by the chaplains themselves being deeply present to those who have been stricken by loss.

4. Process, Not Content, Is Key

When the focus of a chaplain is on the *content* of the person expressing grief, debate and apology take over. Avoiding this path entails making an important distinction between what is said and what is meant. This distinction changes the way chaplains respond.

Focus on the content, for example, means that the question "Why has God stricken me?" is managed by a careful explanation of why God doesn't do such terrible things; this, in turn, is heard as a chaplain's judgment that the patient is lacking in faith. Focus on the *process* creates an opportunity for the chaplain and patient to explore together what it means to be overcome by such powerful forces of weakness and illness.[3] Focus on content means that the desperate statement "I wish it was all over" needs a corrective of medicinal trust in "someone else's plan." Focus on *process* hears this statement as an opportunity to reflect on the meaning of death and uncover in the patient helpful ways to prepare for death.

Likewise, the chaplain may hear families engage in recrimination of themselves—for example, focusing on ways in which they could have been instrumental in preventing this death. Such expressions of guilt rarely address the facts but do indicate an uncomfortableness with the powerlessness people experience under the force of death. This kind of guilt or sense of being punished can be even stronger when the one who dies is an infant or child. Focus on the process hears words of guilt and recrimination as a lament of helplessness, sometimes even abandonment.

Mistaken focus on content wants to solve the major decisions which families face in times of loss (e.g. "What shall we do about income?" "Should we put mother in a nursing home?" etc.). On the other hand, focus on the process recognizes that the voicing of these questions about the future are frequently an expression of fear, helplessness or fatigue. The problems do not need immediate solutions. At times, chaplains may need to encourage families directly in taking time to sort out the major questions and decisions which seem to be on top of them.

Exceptions always exist, and one exception in which chaplains need to be with families in making a "content" decision is in the donation of organs to medical facilities. With the increased number of states making provision for this generosity through living wills, drivers' licenses, etc., the need to make a decision without knowing the will of the deceased has decreased. Yet chaplains will still face this moment of decision where they are challenged to balance compassion for the grieving with a care for those who continue to suffer through illness. In these dialogues, chaplains continue to remain respectful and compassionate, for they know that a painful decision is in process; once families have made decisions, even if different from the chaplain's or hospital's wishes, it is vital to continue in the mode of being a ministerial presence.

5. Like Lament, Expressed Grief Is a Witness of Trust

Jesus' cry of abandonment on the cross is rarely treated as a loss of faith. Likewise, the cry of abandonment in Psalm 51 is regularly seen as a legitimate form of prayer in our Judeo-Christian tradition. Such lament was a regular course in the menu of psalmic prayer which the Hebrew Testament records. Here is prayer which hurts, which witnesses to a people's experience of exile and abandonment, and which leaves hearers hanging on an edge of disorientation. What is its value? Its value is in the process more than the content. In these prayers of lament we come face-to-face with a people who can "bare their souls" before God without fear of reprisal or punishment. We come face-to-face with a people expressing trust on the deepest and most difficult level of their lives. Their lament is an expression of trust.[4]

I was once ejected from a hospital room by a patient who vociferously expressed his anger about the way I dressed; judging in his particular case that a very direct response was necessary, I thanked him for trusting me by voicing his anger in such a deep way. While his natural pride would not permit him to rescind the demand that I leave that day, his surprise at my response motivated a weak invitation to return on another day.

The response of chaplains lets the grieving know that their expression of lament is acceptable. Chaplains do not try to resolve the pain nor do they offer remedies and corrections. The chaplains' hospitality toward lament enables the value of the lament to be uncovered, i.e. the response provides an environment whereby that lament may be experienced as a moment of trust, confidence, or even deep faith. Chaplains rarely bring hope to another, but often uncover that hope over time.

6. The Pain of Grief Needs a Companion

As earlier noted, chaplains are aware of how important it is to be a personal companion to those who grieve. The grieving find some assurance in the awareness that they are not alone. Yet their pain remains unique, and few can identify with the pain in the same way that the grieving person does. The way in which chaplains "befriend" those who are grieving is by being as deeply present to the people as they can.

In their presence as a companion, chaplains cannot take away the pain or the grief, but they can listen carefully enough so that the grieving know they are not alone. An inviting presence reduces the fear of those grieving and allows them opportunity to voice their pain without embarrassment or fear of reprisal.

Such a chaplain-companion evidences patience, compassion and hope. Patience allows the expression of grief to unfold in its unique way with the conviction that a deep mystery is being unraveled. Compassion meets those who grieve on the level of affect; although chaplains can never experience the grief as mourners do, their own attentiveness to the experience of sad feeling says that they are willing to "suffer with" another. The hope which the chaplain brings to the encounter is a confidence in the present moment; in other words, chaplains do not offer hope as a future goal or remedy, but they identify, when appropriate, the value of expressions of grief which are being shared.

7. Prayer Connects

Prayer has a most meaningful character for those who grieve when it flows generally from the encounter with mystery which the grieving experience and specifically from the human encounter and time which the chaplain shares with those in grief. Prayer does not serve when it appears meaninglessly interjected into a painful experience or when it is used to cover over the chaplain's own inability to respond humanly to those going through loss.

Ritual or rote prayers with which the grieving are familiar provide calm access to an experience of connecting with the divine because those who grieve can easily pray in familiar ways. But such prayers need to be accompanied by prayer which speaks directly in the situation, prayer which gives a "holy" voice to some of the feelings which people normally attribute to be "bad" or "negative."

Frequently chaplains will be called on to voice in prayer what is being experienced. Chaplains may also find it appropriate to give people an opportunity to offer prayer in their own words. When introducing such prayer, the chaplain's own prayer serves as an example, and hence is most helpful when the language is concrete and specific (not theological or abstract). The texts of scripture are a primary resource for chaplains because scripture itself voices prayer in ways which are connected to the stories of people's lives. Consequently, chaplains are familiar with the range of texts in scripture and make use of the texts to give voice to the experience of grief, never to provide a facile answer to pain nor to hide the chaplains' speechlessness.

Chaplains will also want to be clear that it is all right if some or all do not wish to pray aloud. When chaplains know the person who has died, their own prayer might very well include some expression of gratitude for the gift which the now deceased person brought to the chaplains themselves.

8. Silence Is an Empowering Word

Chaplains who are at home with silence and meditation in their own lives will also be comfortable with silences among those who grieve. Such moments of silence are not rare at all. However, especially since the American culture provides few opportunities for pause in "input reception," many people can find silences to be upsetting or awkward, especially if chaplains come across as uneasy with silence.

Chaplains send signals about their level of comfortability with silence. When they are rushed, talk too much or too loudly, or respond without thinking, they encourage an uncomfortability. When they give evidence of patience, when they think about their responses, and when they are calm in their demeanor, they open others to the mystery of silence.

Silence in an encounter with the faces of grief offers chaplains a moment to process internally what they are hearing. Silence admits to those who grieve that we share a limited character which has no ready answers for loss. Silence permits those who share it to become bonded on a level of mystery. Silence also permits mourners a time to reflect upon the experience they are undergoing; it is a kind of intermission in the midst of intensity. All in all, silence says, "Clocks are not important, but you are, and this moment is important."

9. When the Grievers Take Leave . . .

At the frequent times when the chaplain's encounter with grief occurs in one-time settings, the chaplain sets a stage for the transition which will go on outside of the hospital. To assist in such transition, chaplains should be aware of the various faith communities which comprise the neighboring areas, especially if the family and friends involved are not too well-connected. If chaplains have already set the stage for the expression of grief in a faith context, it becomes all the more important that this faith-filled expression be permitted to continue. In addition, however, chaplains may wish to have available an ability to refer to other resources of which grievers might make use.

The time of leave-taking after death often presents an opportunity to face the body of the deceased for a final time. Whatever the chaplains believe about the value of this practice, it remains most important to be attentive to the needs of the particular family. In situations where the chaplain is familiar with the family or where the chaplain is qualified to assess the unspoken needs of the family, gentle recommendations may be in order.

Unless the relationship of the grieving with the chaplain is structured so that there is a connection with the family when they leave the hospital, chaplains will want to be aware of their own experience of transition. They entrust the grieving to their respective communi-

ties and they take time to process the experience
themselves.

10. Chaplains Grieve, Too

The experience of loss on the part of chaplains needs
constant attention which the chaplains themselves can
take measures to assure. Their loss is experienced in
their identification with those who grieve, in the death
of patients whom they have come to value, in the leave-
taking with families after the death of a loved one, in the
lack of expressed gratitude for their ministry.

The very first step in being attentive to one's own
grief is to make the honest admission of humanity to
oneself. Chaplains must constantly remember that they
are not immune to pain, sadness and powerlessness.

Such an admission, however, is only a first step.
Chaplains help themselves when they spend time in
quiet reflection whose purpose is to identify the stages
of grief which they experience. This reflection builds
their self-awareness and reduces the possibility that
chaplains will only be ministering to themselves in situations of grief. Another reason for careful reflection is
that chaplains are frequently more "in tune" with the
end of the story and are apt to look for the sunrise in a
dark experience. Identification of their own process of
grief helps them to realize that, as faithful as they may
be, there are also important moments of darkness which
precede the passage into promise.

Since they cannot be expected to experience their
grief alone, chaplains also need mentors or companions
with whom they can voice that grief. No loss is trivial

for anyone. What chaplains remember about the grief of others stands equally true for themselves.

∞

Notes/Suggested Readings

[1] Charles Meyer (1991). *Surviving Death: A Practical Guide to Caring for the Dying and Bereaved.* Mystic: Twenty-Third Publications. In this book Meyer identifies a number of "theological slogans" which are often misconstrued as faithful responses to the experience of grief, pp. 81–91.

[2] This volume is a helpful resource for developing an understanding of the way in which various faith and cultural traditions view death. Kenneth Kramer (1988). *The Sacred Art of Dying: How World Religions Understand Death.* New York: Paulist Press.

[3] Stanley Hauerwas (1990). *Naming the Silences: God, Medicine and the Problem of Suffering.* Grand Rapids: William B. Eerdmans Publishing Co. Focusing primarily on the death of children, Hauerwas attempts to discover the meaning within illness and death and the way in which "the God whom Christians worship" gives voice to the pain of people in grief.

[4] In this book Walter Brueggemann provides an excellent resource for understanding the role of the psalms and especially lament. Walter Brueggemann (1984). *The Message of the Psalms: A Theological Commentary.* Minneapolis: Augsburg.

5

Guilt and Shame

William J. Sneck, S.J., Ph.D.

∾

1. Distinguishing Between Guilt and Shame

At a recent workshop focused on the "hard" emotions and dealing with one's hurt, anger, and guilt, I was attempting to tease out succinctly distinctions between guilt and shame. A woman participant successfully summed up my presentation in words I wish I had thought of: "You mean that guilt is feeling, 'I *made* a mistake,' and shame feels like 'I *am* a mistake'?"

Such a simple statement profoundly presents many differences between these two painful, difficult human experiences. Keeping her words in mind while reading my words should clarify how guilt and shame can resemble each other (the element of "mistake") and yet are so disparate. Her suggestion provides clues for responding to persons struggling with each experience.

2. Hearing What a Patient Is Presenting— Establishing Rapport

First place in importance when establishing rapport with a patient—or more accurately, perhaps, as an aspect of grounding a counseling relationship—goes to really attending to, really hearing what a sufferer is communicating. In guilt and shame, inner states that resemble each other and are often described in similar-sounding words, the helping professional is challenged

48

to discern just what is the presenting problem. (Of course, real live persons' issues often really are intertwined, but it helps to know what to listen for, so that the elements of guilt and shame can be separated for the sake of analysis and treatment suggestions.)

3. Two Dimensions of Guilt

Suppose that the essence of the person's communication is the sense that "I made a mistake." This sounds like an issue of guilt and needs to be explored along two dimensions at least: thoughts/feelings and health/unhealth. That is, the listener may wonder whether the speaker moves more comfortably in the cognitive or the affective realm and whether the guilt is healthy (and to be honored) or unhealthy (and to be uprooted.)

4. Assisting a "Thinker's" or "Feeler's" Struggles with Guilt

Take a common but uncommonly painful situation: a busy husband (whether factory-worker or yuppie lawyer) forgets his wedding anniversary. After a blow-up at home, efforts toward reconciliation seem to get nowhere. Because alienation seems to be growing from other issues, he seeks assistance in counseling. While relationship concerns are your and his primary focus, dealing with guilt becomes part of your conversation. One sort of man might speak aloud his frustration at not achieving his self-professed ideals, standards, and inner norms, one of which is "I must remember dates of significance to my loved ones." This fellow, more of a "thinker" than a "feeler," could be invited to reflect on whether he is holding his principle in too absolute a way, or whether he needs to balance a principle like this with another on self-forgiveness, or whether he should take a broader view of his life-pattern, schedule of work and play, and style of interacting with his wife and family.

Imagine the same situation, with the man saddened, maybe grief-stricken, at the pain he caused his beloved. To this man, her hurt means ever so much more than his own forgetfulness. This man's locus of problems is the heart more than the head, and he must be responded to accordingly. It will be profitable for him to perform a "feeling inventory" orally with you, in writing at home, and interpersonally with his spouse. Teach him to explore the concrete circumstances of his life (as in the previous case), but by focusing on their impact on himself and others, he can achieve perspective on his guilt. A context will grow around the incident such that its seriousness can be objectively (and still feelingly) weighed, depending on whether this event is part of a pattern, or stands alone. According to whether the client lives in his or her mind or heart, a counselor will move to locate and interpret the guilt. It is most important for the counselor to be aware of his or her own preferred realm of discourse, so that, like a dancer, one can follow the lead of the partner even if the steps are unpracticed.

5. Evaluating Healthy vs. Unhealthy Guilt

The other dimension to ponder concerns whether the guilt is healthy or unhealthy. "Healthy" guilt may seem a contradiction in terms, especially to a chaplain where categories like "sin" and "blame" are harsh and value-ladened. Unless schooled to write off selfish impulses and behaviors as resulting totally from the environmental conditioning of home, poverty, role models, deprivation, etc., most persons instinctively, if not very deeply, possess awareness of inner inclinations toward the good and away from evil. Named "conscience" by the rational tradition of western moral philosophy and theology, this inner voice of responsibility prohibits intentions of wrongdoing, and follows actions undertaken contrary to its mandate with punishing thoughts and feelings of guilt. Consequently, conscience, and its offspring guilt, should be valued as gifts of the Almighty, as guides on the journey of life that, like silent brambles at the roadside, warn us at night when we wander off the true path because we have forgotten or ignored our values or temporarily pursued false lights.

If guilt is in principle potentially healthy, how does one discern whether or not one's guilt or the guilt of one's patient deserves attention? The criterion of proportionality comes to mind; thus one *should* feel guilty and judge oneself blameworthy *more* or *less* in terms of the degree of the offense contemplated or committed, the objective seriousness of the wrong involved. Healthy guilt occurs when the depth of emotion or the sting of self-critical thoughts parallels the degree of evil as judged by a reflective consensus of informed members of the community. Thus, in American society, varying degrees of guilt would be deemed of relatively appropriate intensity if one felt *somewhat* guilty for telling a white lie to escape minor embarrassment; felt *more* guilty for stealing items from one's place of employment; felt *very* guilty for consistently underpaying one's employees; suffered *extreme* guilt after perjuring oneself under oath.

6. Treatment Strategy

Lack of proportionate guilt at either end of the scale indicates pathologies, but of different types. Should the rare telling of a white lie—or the commitment of an offense of similar magnitude—generate paroxysms of guilt, impair relaxed functioning, or cause one to spend much time pondering one's degree of guilt and worrying about one's eternal salvation, a scrupulous conscience could be the culprit. Such a conscience spawns *un*healthy guilt. The problem here is not moral but psychological, a form of obsessive-compulsive neurosis. Unless a chaplain had special psychological or psychiatric training in dealing with anxiety disorders, he or she should work with another professional or make a referral. The goal is to stand up to and resist acting on such guilt.

On the other hand, were one's sense of guilt negligible or lacking after perjury or some similarly serious offense, the counselor should raise the suspicion of dealing with a person afflicted with an antisocial personality disorder. For such a client, tough love is the order of the day rather than, say, unconditional acceptance and warmth. Shoring up a weak or sagging conscience would be a favor to the client and to society. Here one's conscience is unhealthy because it seems unable to perform its guiding function and stir up good guilt.

Stated simply, healthy guilt ought to be attended to; toxic guilt should be counterattacked. When a guilt-laden thought or emotion occurs *before* an action, one should be encouraged habitually to obey one's conscience if the guilt is evaluated as healthy. If healthy guilt *follows* an action, one should seek interpersonal reconciliation, and intrapersonally one might pray for healing through genuine contrition and repentance. If, however, the guilt is judged toxic, one should make every effort not to behave according to its authoritarian demands, and should attempt to understand and remove the cause of this irrational guilt through reflection, prayer, counseling, or spiritual direction.

Let me add a clarification about discerning the relative health or toxicity of guilt. While the criterion of community consensus serves as a useful yardstick, the ultimate norm remains one's individual conscience, correctly informed, and in dialogue with the Holy Spirit of God. A frequently occurring reminder of this point nowadays is the demonstration of non-violent protesters who, through civil disobedience, deliberately break human law in their proclamation of adherence to divine law. Whether the cause is anti-nuclear disarmament, anti-war protests, environmental protection, animal rights, or anti-abortion, groups of persons deliberately flout legal order to urge society to rethink its adherence to the status quo in contemporary neuralgic areas of controversy. Just as society instructs the individual through custom, education, traditions, the media, so too do prophetic individuals teach their fellow citizens to examine their collective conscience about who is really guilty at deeper levels of moral observance. Thus the establishment of right thinking, right behavior, and right moral reasoning is never a once-and-for-all given, but results from the ongoing dynamic tension between community and citizen, whether that community is civil or ecclesiastical.

7. Characteristics of Shame

We return once again from the streets to the patient's room where a chaplain is energetically trying to understand and assist a patient. Though hearing thoughts and feelings of guilt as the main focus of their discussion, the chaplain senses shame in the client as well. When one engages in the process of judging one's action, thoughts, or speech as morally reprehensible, one may also feel shame, often as a by-product. It is perhaps accurate to say that, experientially, there is a greater variety of shame-feelings than of guilt-feelings. Though guilty thoughts and feelings accompany a premeditated or actual violation of a moral norm or dictate of conscience, shame derives from any incongruence between behavior and one's idealized self or ego-ideal. The discrepancy may not even involve morality. If the reader will excuse a personal example, I vividly recall now, more than thirty years after the event, the only time I came up to bat with three men on base and two out in the bottom of the ninth inning during a seminary championship baseball game. Like Mighty Casey, but without his vocalized bravado, I too struck out. The stinging shame of that moment is still remembered, but with amusement now, and without the painful chagrin, humiliation, embarrassment, mortification and fury of the moment, all augmented by the averted eyes of my disappointed teammates.

Thus shame can involve the gaze of significant others and may result from any behavioral departure from one's preferred self. Take another non-moral example: a seminary companion was extremely shy in his early days with us, and would blush when he met new people. As he was a member of an apostolic order, his ideal was to become comfortable in meeting and serving people, and his blush signaled his discomfort at not yet achieving this goal.

The facial blush provides a good bodily symbol of the inner shame and embarrassment experienced. (Guilt, of course, also has its physiological correlates in averted eyes, garbled speech, sweaty palms and armpits, but the vivid blood-red mark of shame draws the attention of its bearer and of his companions.) Shame can show even if others are unaware of the reason for the inner conflict: people can be congratulated for winning the highest achievement in any field of endeavor, and their blush may signify not embarrassment before unexpected publicity, but knowledge that they cheated and used dishonest or exploitive means to get to the top.

With or without the blush, however, shame will be felt whenever I behave or act in a way that does not fit my sense of who I am, or who my best self is. Healthy shame prevents self-inflation. As a normal human emotion, shame is good and healthy because by it we are reminded of our limits and our growth-needs and potential. Shame prevents self-inflation when we forget or ignore our actual achievements, or sinful past and present, all that we have yet to repent and correct. Though we often fight the awareness, healthy shame reminds us that we can and do make mistakes, that we need human and divine assistance, that maturity does not mean macho control and independence, but a respectful and shared interdependence. Though unpleasant, healthy shame provides a psychological foundation for humility and issues in spirituality.

8. Toxic Shame Means "I Am Deficient"

Thus far, healthy shame. Unhealthy shame is most pithily expressed in the statement quoted earlier, "I *am* a mistake." Shame dehumanizes when it evolves into a state of being, into one's whole sense of self-as-flawed. To endure shame as characterizing one's identity means believing that one's being is blameworthy, that one is, deep down, deficient as a human being.

Unhealthy shame, like unhealthy guilt, is more often a psychological problem than a moral difficulty. Even in a social setting, and with or without any training in counseling, we all have met persons who, in just a few minutes of conversation, reveal a deep, thick vein of self-hatred just below their psychic surface. Contemporary retreat master, writer, and spiritual director George Aschenbrenner has noted that *the* most pervasive modern heresy is "I am no good." (Personal communication.) Milder variants of this unhealthy shame are: a negative self-image that clashes with the esteem and respect held by the sufferer's co-workers and colleagues; a sense that one is forever the losing player in life's game of "Never Enough," wherein one feels unable to ever win affection from or please any of one's family members; workaholism, a compulsive effort driven by a need for approval from others because inner self-acceptance and self-love are lacking.

Much more severe forms of unhealthy shame clog the character structure of survivors of child abuse, whether verbal, physical, or sexual. Inevitably the victim rather than the perpetrator blames himself or herself for having occasioned, invited, demanded the abuse through his or her naughty or seductive behavior. Often memories of the events are blocked, and healing happens only with patient psychotherapeutic intervention.

The most severe outcome of unhealthy shame occurs, of course, in suicide where tormented individuals enact their belief in their total depravity by blotting it out. Consider Judas' fate . . .

9. A Developmental Perspective on Guilt and Shame

Looking at shame and guilt from a developmental perspective adds insight on the origin of these experiences. Following Erik Erikson (1963), John Bradshaw (1988) has helpfully analyzed the different dynamics underlying shame and guilt. Shame arises earlier than guilt. During Erikson's second psychosocial stage (age fifteen months to three years), the major task confronting the developing child is to learn to balance autonomy and shame/doubt. As children begin to walk and explore their environment, they must slowly separate from their primary parental figures with whom they have established, it is hoped, a relationship of trust during the first stage. Grasping, smelling, tasting, pushing limits, youngsters develop a growing sense of autonomy bounded by doubt and shame beyond which they may not safely venture. During this delicate period, abuse easily tips the equation in the direction of self-doubt and shame.

The next and third psychosocial stage of development, according to Erikson (1963), is the balance between initiative and guilt, which is ordinarily achieved between the third and the sixth year. Guilt is built upon internalized rules and develops later than does shame. Developmentally, guilt is more mature than shame. Guilt does not impinge directly upon one's identity or lessen one's deepest sense of personal worth, as shame can.

10. Assisting the Suffering

Ministering to those afflicted with shame and guilt can be enriched by consulting a colleague trained in psychiatry, psychology, or social work, and it is from such a perspective that this essay has been penned. Yet a chaplain must never forget his or her own distinct theological and spiritual tradition when assisting a patient.

St. Paul had tried to earn his way into personal holiness through works of the law, and it was only when he experienced the "unconditional positive regard" of Jesus, his Savior, that he was able to exult in newfound freedom. Extending such love and acceptance by standing in Jesus' place can similarly bring peace to the shame- and guilt-ridden.

St. Peter betrayed his master, but his looking Jesus in the eye and weeping bitterly are a model of acts of repentance and reconciliation for evil deeds.

Using imagery and reminding clients of biblical stories with which they can identify can point clients toward healthy transformation of their guilt and shame into opportunities for growth.

∽

Suggested Readings

Bradshaw, John (1988). *Healing the Shame that Binds You*. Deerfield Beach: Health Communications, Inc.

Erikson, Erik (1963). *Childhood and Society*. New York: W.W. Norton.

Glaser, John W. (1971). "Conscience and Superego: A Key Distinction," *Theological Studies* 32, pp. 30–47.

Kelley, Kathleen E. (ed.) (1980). *Guilt: Issues of Emotional Living in an Age of Stress* (The Fifth Psychotheological Symposium). Whitinsville: Affirmation Books.

Lewis, Helen B. (1971). *Shame and Guilt in Neurosis.* New York: International Universities Press.

Menninger, Karl (1973). *Whatever Became of Sin?* New York: Hawthorn Books, Inc.

Shelton, Charles M. (1990). *Morality of the Heart: A Psychology for the Christian Moral Life.* New York: Crossroad.

Soboson, Jeffrey (1982). *Guilt and the Christian: A New Perspective.* Chicago: Thomas More Press.

Westphal, Merald (1984). *God, Guilt and Death: An Existential Phenomenology of Religion.* Bloomington: Indiana University Press.

6

Working with the "Chronologically-Gifted"

Edward R. Killackey, M.M., M.S.

∾

Introduction

Titling the chapter "Working with the 'Chronologically-Gifted' '' may seem to some to be an exercise in hyperbole. There is pastoral intent in being reluctant to focus on the word "elderly." Until recently the vocabulary of life-span development lent a negative tone to growing old. Though the tonality was not overtly negative, it was restrictive and stereotypical at best. Balance will be restored by reflecting on the aging process as a gift—of tenure and chronology—to the present day interactions of the generations. If the chaplain does not exorcise himself or herself of culture-bound assessments and expectations of the elderly, pastoral action in their behalf will be disabled and incongruent.

There is a new vitality in the field of gerontology. It was not always so. The field and its prophetic personalities had to strive for a proper place alongside related fields of medicine, psychiatry and pastoral counseling. The underservice of the generations of the young-old and old-old was excused by facetiously responding that the elderly themselves were resistant to the services and programs offered. Pastoral care had a better track record in this regard but it too fell short of the needs of the elderly.

These are now good times. Literature on the elderly abounds in articles and in entire journals focusing on the aging. Conferences and institutes on religion and gerontology are now frequent. In 1991 the National Board for Certified Counselors inaugurated certification criteria for a National Certified Gerontological Counselor. New energies and leadership have transformed the activities and advocacy of members of national organizations by the mature person. Lacunae in medical and theological education have been filled by curricula and internships focusing on the mature generations.

∽

1. Awareness and Involvement

Aging and the human spirit now has pride of place in the form of the disciplines, organizations, professions, and in social structures. There is much more to do. The happy task will prosper if chaplains enhance their gerontological competencies. How? By active participation in professional organizations, by continuing education at conferences and institutes and by being a herald in their own work environment for the chronologically gifted. There is no better time to so engage oneself.

A note of pastoral concern. Boredom is an unfamiliar experience of the chaplain. Demands on the chaplains—scheduled worship services, mentoring of the pastoral team, scheduling and nurturing of volunteers, supervision and paperwork—all generate a vortex of harried activity which often prevents pastoral contact with the person. That same flurry of activity gnaws away at time and place for professional development and pastoral reflection. The chaplain, an evoker of God's word in healing environments, often finds little time for that task of evocation. His or her interiority and interpersonal skills fall victim to the stress of scheduling and appointments. The chaplain, called to be light, becomes a candle. Chronologically gifted patients are usually the first victims of oversight and underservice. Paradoxically, pastoral care of the elderly will gift the chaplain with fresh and perduring insights into the asceticism of time and the management of pastoral presence.

2. The Chaplain Must Be a Collaborator

The field of geriatrics has, in these days, attracted human service professionals of high quality. Doctors, physician assistants, nurses, social workers, administrators and managers—people of vision, competency and compassion—now fill the ranks of health care and spiritual care activity. The continuity of care is enhanced by home aides, practical nurses, security personnel and food service personnel implementing that vision. Ironically, some of the best diagnoses and assessments are made by the latter. All of the above are excellent sources of referral for the chaplain. Care and healing of the chronologically gifted hinges on the blend of scientific and humanistic attentiveness toward patients. For that reason, chaplaincy today is a call to collaborative ministry.

What an opportunity for the chaplain to pursue and model a collaborative mode of pastoral care. Matthias Neuman, writing in *Church* (Winter 1988), notes:

We could look at four aspects of collaborative ministry. First, we need to articulate a vision, a theology, or theoretical formulation of its religious roots and importance. Second, people need practical lessons in the organizational dynamics required for successful cooperation. Third, there is the shaping of one's own ministerial expectations and practical dealing with the obstacles one might encounter. Finally, a fourth segment of investigation, the one we take up here, seeks to formulate a spirituality for collaborative ministry.

The common good of the elderly mandates that professional turf battles give way to collaboration. The healing context of our tasks should prod us to be tolerant of competing visions and to be respectful of the high energy level of the "visionaries." Turf and positive disregard contaminate the healing environment. An uncollaborative lifestyle can be a major source of stress. Compromises have to be worked out between the clinical and the pastoral. In so many ways they are complementary and enhance each other. Accepting the necessary polarity between the clinical and the pastoral is the challenge to all of us. The chaplain should model the needed collaboration.

3. The Chaplain Should Be Assertive

Huh? You just told us to be collaborative. Now you are urging us to be assertive. Contradictory, isn't it? It need not be so.

There is a hemorrhaging within the disciplines, and, as paradigms pale, the struggle toward interdisciplinary caring of the elderly can easily make contestants of health care professionals. What clashes arise these days?

- A clash of visions. Secular institutions now articulate mission statements. Those of us who have a proprietary attitude to the word "mission" are threatened.

- The elderly are recipients of services that deeply touch their lives—living wills, durable power of attorney, advice about codes and other bio-ethical dilemmas. The elderly, rooted in faith practice, are urged to participate in non-denominational, corporate programs of inspiration and motivation. In all of the above, it would seem that the domain of pastoral care has been encroached upon.

In these days it is important that the chaplain be assertive. The chaplain should shape, in a collaborative style, a pastoral vision with his or her co-workers. They should proclaim it, pursue it and reiterate the vision at staff and management meetings. There is a specificity to the tasks of the chaplain. Waffling on this needed specificity—failing to assert it—will be a disservice to the elderly. It is not uncommon for mission statements to repose in file cabinets with no pastoral care workers claiming ownership or responsibility for their implementation.

The polarities, seemingly intrusive, are necessary in today's health care environment. The focus group—the elderly—will, in time, benefit from the widening involvement of human services personnel in the latter-life stage ministries. The chaplain who is threatened by this new reality will too readily assume the role of contestant. Healing postures will be displaced by strife. Self-defeating behaviors will postpone an exciting future of collaboration in meeting the overlapping needs of the elderly.

Need a model for the needed assertiveness? The qualities of Mary, the first disciple, are called for. Her place in salvation history was an inter-testamentary one. She was called to be a woman of transition, a straddler of covenants. In living out her life of discipleship she balanced the traits of hospitality to the new with her assertiveness of the traditional. Not a bad model . . .

4. The Chaplain Should Be Imaginative

The *loci* for the action of the Spirit are many: assembly, table, road, hills, edges, interruptions, threesomes, acts of re-membering, risk and folly. Pastoral care of the elderly is truly a locus laden with the freedom to imagine. We have been served well by the editors of the *Journal of Pastoral Care* in this regard.

Years ago, it was Urban T. Holmes, III, who boldly asserted:

> The fundamental issue in ministry is the recovery of a sense of enchantment and the ability to be enchanting.

Holmes ended his book *The Future Shape of Ministry* with a call for ministry to exercise its imagination. His *Ministry and Imagination* is an intuitive response to that original call.

The pastoral care of the elderly is an enviable place to be so as to provoke the action of the Spirit, for several reasons:

- There are few models to shape a spirituality of aging for those enjoying extended life. Pastoral

theology offers no paradigms. Pastoral praxis
seems to be befuddled by the happy task. What an
opportunity for creative improvisation!

- Pastoral care personnel enjoy an autonomy from
constricting and risk-less environments that serve
others. We can, without constraint, entertain a
new way of being pastorally present to the elderly. We are called to be futurists. And the future
we labor in is not an unknown.

- Our "pride of place" situates us in the lives of
those who have actually had the experience of aging. The needed pastoral praxis will flow from
hearing their story. We do not need to construct
intellectual theories about it.

5. Seeing the Elderly Developmentally

One hopes for a life cycle-minded chaplain who applies her or his imagination to the task of expanding
Stage VIII of Erik Erikson's esteemed theory of life cycle. There is much more to extended life than the polarity of integrity/despair. We need to set aside our dog-
matic symmetry of thought about the elderly and speak
to wonder, play, passion and creativity in their lives.
Maturity in no way forecloses psychosocial or psycho-
sexual growth nor does it declare a moratorium on the
ego's task of integrity and identity. Aging may well be a
medium for creative exploration in future styles of spirituality, worship and ministry. So much rich thought,
theory and action has flowed from applying the epige-
netic principle to childhood, adolescence and adult-

hood. What richness awaits us if we imaginatively apply that same principle to those now enjoying extended life?

6. The Chaplain Should Be Ordinary

Being "ordinary" is an act of imagination—and a locus for the activity of the Spirit. Fruits of the Spirit in the pastoral life of the chaplain would be: being as your most important act; availability; the shedding of outer attitudes and behaviors that belie mere professionalism; muting the visage of harriedness—and so many other attributes and traits that make us less ordinary. The ordinal, the "orders of the day," often subvert the healing relationship.

7. The Elderly Are More Than an Object of Service

The chronologically gifted are besieged by those who want to do things for them. Being an object of service by others is often disabling and depersonalizing. The chaplain, of all health care professionals, owes the aging generations the gifts of listening, attending, empathy, genuineness and concreteness. How incarnational! The elderly need surcease from initiative behaviors and initiative conditions.

Robert F. Joyce, in his article "Being as Our Most Important Act," reminds us:

Peace in self and society comes from creatively listening hearts. Centering ourselves in meaningful activity is a crucial part of the receptive power of a peaceful presence. But, if we are to be enriched in our conversations, behaviors, prayer, mediation, and simple asceticism, we need to improve how we center ourselves.

Joyce concludes his reflection:

> Being is your most important act. In some
> sense, it is your only act. All other acts or activi-
> ties stem from and are expressive of this dy-
> namic being that you are.

8. The Chaplain Should Be Advocacy-Minded

There is need of optimum participation by the aging
generations in the decisions affecting their lives. Justice
calls us to engage our energies in assisting the elderly
gain access to the nation's resources. In U.S. culture the
chaplain is in a unique position to translate his or her
solidarity with the elderly into advocacy. *Sollicitudo
Rei Socialis* (1988), putting flesh to *Gaudium et spes*
(1965), calls us to socio-political mission. The church is
called to (1) prophetic word, (2) symbolic witness and (3)
political action. Solidarity and at-one-ment urge us to
insert gospel content and values into the cultural
context.

The chaplain reads the "signs of the times" as they
impact on the elderly. Some of those signs are:

- Challenge of elder abuse and neglect
- Long-term care reform
- Poverty of elderly females
- Older women in the labor force
- Cutbacks in Medicare
- High health care inflation
- Declining availability of private pensions
- Issues of generational equity
- Inclusionary strategies for low-income and minor-
  ity elders

The chaplain has a pivotal role in the health care system and must necessarily be both participant and shaper of public policy. There is a social ministry component to chaplaincy to the aging. Training in legislative advocacy and policy analysis is offered by every organization or agency we belong to. We are surrounded by networks seeking our participation.

9. Be a Model of Compassion

The chaplain is a model of compassion. What a happy day it will be when the chaplain is a model of justice advocacy for the elderly. The immediacy of their pastoral experience with both elderly and care-givers equips them well to become spokepersons in the arena of public policy. The legislative arena is an environment that needs to be inhabited by chaplains. Jesus the healer focused on those denied advocacy and deprived of access to community resources. Justice advocacy should be a constitutive element of the job description of every chaplain.

10. The Chaplain Should Be Aware of Care-Givers

An outstanding character trait of Jesus was his intuitive awareness of those "on the edges." His peripheral vision was acute. Gospel stories are replete with the phrase "While Jesus was on his way . . ." In the ordinary day of the chaplain his or her path will cross with the care-giver. Such persons may be in the medical professional or even in management. They often come into our purview with need—often unexpressed. The friendliness, the openness, the availability of the chaplain often triggers meaningful encounter. It may only be a greeting, a short conversation, or a moment. Evangelization often takes place in moments. A playful reading of the gospels depicting the ordinary days of Jesus' ministry clues us in to a sorely needed ministry—the ministry of interruption. The chaplain, open to spontaneous encounter, graces the life of the professional and compounds the healing of the elderly when he or she "raps with the staff." We do have a strategic role to play with the professional care-giver. Your welcoming visage and willingness to be interrupted will draw those "on the edges" into your presence. Chaplains, by training, if not by nature, are intuitive people.

In addition to professional care-givers, there are family care-givers. They are often stress-filled. Being in your presence may be the only possible pastoral support they can experience. They may wish to do several things: pray with you, present their stress, or merely verbalize their powerlessness. Being available to care-givers is hardly a peripheral task for the chaplain. Being available reconciles, strengthens familial ties and builds small communities. Human affect provokes pastoral effect.

∾

Conclusion

Our tasks as evokers of God's word and healing take place in three "orbits": (1) interiority, (2) interpersonal and (3) institutions. These orbits act back on us; we, in turn, act on them. Pastoral care of the chronologically gifted causes these orbits to intersect and, at times, to coincide. And these orbits collide!

As emphasized, the elderly need chaplains who are collaborative, assertive, imaginative, ordinary and advocacy-minded. It is just as important for the chaplain to be aware of these "orbits." Interiority will grace the actions of the chaplain with the needed negative capability. The interpersonal is already a core skill of the pastoral care agent. The new energetic presence of corporations in the health care delivery system gives fresh contextual meaning to the word "institution."

The task of the chaplain? To integrate his or her interiority, interpersonal skills and institutional service with gerontological competencies. The chronologically gifted will be the beneficiaries of that integration.

References

Holmes, Urban T. III (1976). *Ministry and Imagination.* New York: Seabury.

Joyce, Robert E. (1988). "Being Is Our Most Important Act," *Listening: Journal of Religion and Culture,* pp. 115–122.

Myers, Jane E. (1988). *Curriculum Guide: Infusing Gerontological Counseling in Counselor Preparation.* Alexandria: American Association for Counseling and Development.

Neuman, Matthias (1988). "Five Virtues of Collaborative Ministry," *Church* (Winter 1988), p. 10.

Suggested Readings

Clayton, Jean (1991). "Let There Be Life: An Approach to Worship with Alzheimer's Patients and Their Friends," *Journal of Pastoral Care,* Vol. XLV (Summer 1991), No. 2.

Clements, W.M. (ed.) (1989). *Ministry with the Aging.* New York: Haworth Press.

Erikson, Erik H. (1985). *The Life Cycle Completed.* New York: Norton.

Lapsley, James N. (1985). "Pastoral Care and Counseling of the Aging," *Clinical Handbook of Pastoral Counseling.* New York: Paulist Press.

Myers, Jane E. (ed.) (1990). "Techniques for Counseling Older Persons," *Journal of Mental Health Counseling,* Vol. 12, No. 3 (July 1990). Newbury Park: Sage Periodicals Press.

Seeber, James J. (ed.) (1990). "Spiritual Maturity in Later Years," *Journal of Religious Gerontology,* Vol. 7, No. 172. New York: Haworth Press.

Wicks, Robert J. (1990). "The Pastoral Care of . . . Yourself," in *Self-Ministry Through Self-Understanding.* Chicago: Loyola University Press.

7

Dealing with Confrontation

Anthony J. DeConciliis, C.S.C., D.Min., Ph.D.

⁓

There is no better definition for the concept of confrontation in pastoral care and counseling than the words of St. Paul in his letter to the Ephesians (4:15). He says, "Speaking the truth in love, we are to grow up in every way into him who is the head." Confrontation is one of the most difficult skills for chaplains, pastors, and pastoral counselors (referred to as chaplains from now on) to utilize since the skill does not stand alone. It is grounded in the skills of empathy, relationship building, understanding of the inner heart and mind of the one seeking help, and a courageous willingness to engage the other at the depths of his or her being. In the process of confrontation, the person is literally challenged to speak the truth which may have been denied for a long time. As a result of confrontation the covenant between the chaplain and the person is enhanced and brought to a depth of reality wherein the person's covenant with God, others, and self comes to be realized in its fullness. In this way, both the chaplain and the person grow up in mature humanness in the name of him who is head.

In this article, the author summarizes some of the literature related to the concept of confrontation mainly from the pastoral care and counseling perspectives. It will present a few definitions commonly held in the field of counseling and present some guidelines for the use of it in pastoral situations. Since many of the authors suggest that it should only be practiced by caring and competent people, a section will be included on the qualities of those who are entitled to confront and use this highly valuable but delicate skill. Finally, a definition of confrontation will be given which summarizes some of the major issues.

Confrontation: A Pastoral Concept

Wayne Oates (1974), a pioneer in the pastoral counseling movement, suggests that in the counseling relationship, a clear covenant of communication must be established in order to develop an atmosphere of trust and security. This means that the chaplain and the person establish a covenant of mutual responsibility where the two treat each other as persons and not as means to some ulterior ends. In this process, the chaplain-helper participates not only in the difficulties of the person but also in his or her world view and vision of life. The helper strives to understand what the person says and feels so that it means as nearly as possible the same to the helper as it does to the person seeking help. This is usually referred to as empathy which is experienced on both a cognitive and an affective level. It is this empathy experience that gives the chaplain the opportunity to aid the person seeking help to find a clear vision of the conflicts in his or her value system as well as the feelings toward people who represent these values in his or her life. Thus, counseling is a covenant which is based on empathy and mutual responsibility. It is within this covenantal relationship that the chaplain confronts the fantasy and reality of the person which lead to greater maturity in the Lord. The covenant of empathy lays the groundwork and provides the courage where the person is encouraged to confront life itself as it is. As the counseling continues, he suggests that covenants of confession, forgiveness, restitution, and concern follow the covenant of confrontation.

Howard Clinebell (1984) in his famous book, *Basic Types of Pastoral Care and Counseling*, continues the work of Oates. He, like Oates, suggests a five stage process for healing beginning with confrontation. He refers to his stages as: confrontation, confession, forgiveness, restitution/responsible actions (change of destructive behaviors), and reconciliation. He puts confrontation into a reconciliation context wherein the person seeks forgiveness. For him, reconciliation is the path a person can take to move from alienation (from oneself, others, and God) to a state of wholeness. He says, "The epidemic of moral confusion and value distortions in our society is the seedbed within which are bred many of the psychological, psychosomatic, interpersonal, and spiritual problems that bring people to counseling and therapy" (p. 138). So confrontation for Clinebell relates to the person's values and ethics in life.

It is not too much of a stretch to say that counseling is a process wherein the person can re-evaluate values and perspectives about life. From this point of view, the use of confrontation in a pastoral situation is an indispensable skill which involves the authority of the chaplain. Clinebell suggests that chaplains (and all pastoral helpers) have a role in the community as spiritual and ethical leaders/guides. One reason that people come to chaplains is to deal with their cognitive and behavioral distortions. What they seek are not answers or judgments, but to learn skills of self-confrontation. In fact, they seek a modeling behavior from the spiritual guide so that this sense of self-efficacy, a belief in self, can be enhanced for the future.

Guilt and Confrontation

The pastoral discussion of confrontation invariably includes the concept of guilt. Daniels and Horowitz (1984) in their book, *Being and Caring: A Psychology for Living*, define guilt as "my feeling that I'm 'bad' for doing what I'm doing, especially when my action is contrary to my image of how I am expected to behave. I feel guilty when I violate others' standards, my own standards, or standards I've borrowed from others and accepted as my own" (p. 148). Clinebell believes that the inner experience of guilt may set the stage for an openness to constructive confrontation always within a caring atmosphere. The chaplain is faced with the guilt of others in so many ways (especially those who serve in the armed forces or find themselves in crisis situations). It may be found directly in the form of a confession or indirectly in a disguised form as in the denial of destructive behavior due to substance abuse. In these cases, the person is aware, at some level, of the cause of the pain. It may even be intentional. This is in contradistinction to the person who suffers a great deal because of characterological issues. Clinebell calls this type of guilt neurotic as opposed to appropriate. People with neurotic guilt are motivated by compulsive thoughts, and therefore do not usually have as much freedom to make choices. They live with a chronic sense of their sinfulness. This type of guilt is not always amenable to confrontation since the feelings are characterologically ingrained. They may benefit more from intense therapy which is usually not provided by chaplains in pastoral care situations. Confrontation for appropriate guilt can be very helpful. For example, a man who is married reports that he is having an affair with his secretary. In this case, since the individual is aware of his guilt, the chaplain may appropriately make the irresponsible behavior an issue by saying something like, "It seems that you are aware of the hurt your behavior is causing your wife, your secretary, and the families involved. Does it seem that a decision on your part may have to be made to resolve your behavior?" In the process, the person may take a referral to marital therapy. Confrontation thus gives the person an opportunity to seek out the real basis or source of the pain. Again, the goal of confrontation is to help the person to learn the skill of self-confrontation.

Common Definitions of Confrontation in the Literature: A Case for Caring

The following are common definitions found in the counseling literature. In almost every case, the authors stress that confrontation must be used with great care because it is such a potentially powerful technique.

1. Carkhuff and Berenson (1977), two pioneers in the field of counseling skill development, describe confrontation as an *honest experience*. When speaking about therapy in crisis situations, they suggest that "the helper must rely upon his experience with the helpees functioning below a minimally facilitative, self-sustaining level. Usually at this point the helper's most
· effective mode of functioning may involve an honest confrontation with the helpee" (pp. 172–173). An honest experience with a constructive person is lacking for low-level functioning persons who seek assistance in crisis and/or on-going therapy. This person will do anything possible to prevent this honest experience. Fantasy may be preferred to reality. This person may define the honest confrontation as an attack, or a hostile act, since

the person is comfortable with the illusion. It is the authors' contention that if the helper does not acknowledge the crisis, confront it, and in so doing confront the person and himself, the helper's passivity reinforces the person's passivity. The real helper is acting in an honest encounter attempting to provide a means for the person to resolve a crisis. In this case, the helper lets the person know that he is with the person and will do whatever needs to be done to free him or her to choose life. In this context, the resistance to act is broken because of the honest confrontation (pp. 172–175).

2. Osipow, Walsh, and Tosi (1980) suggest that confrontation is the direct expression of *unpleasant events* to the person by the helper and is used by the helper when it is apparent that the person does not want to deal with significant matters. Individuals may, for example, consistently avoid matters that are emotionally laden such as sex, intimacy, homosexuality, and guilt by using various defense mechanisms. The authors suggest that it should be used only when a good solid relationship exists, for a special purpose, with great sensitivity to its effects on the person, and never very frequently (pp. 65–66).

3. In Egan's (1986) model for counseling, he stresses that confrontation is always framed in the context of *responsibility and caring.* For him, it is only one of the skills of challenging. The others include: new perspectives through information sharing, advanced empathy, helper self-sharing, and immediacy. For him, "confrontation is an invitation to examine some form of behavior that seems to be either self-defeating, harmful to others, or both, and to change the behavior if it is

found to be so" (p. 219). What he challenges counselors to find in their communication with the helpee are discrepancies, distortions, evasions, games, tricks, excuse making, and smoke screens. All of these keep the helpees mired in their problem situations. He says that the goal of confrontation is not to strip people of their defenses, but rather to invite clients to challenge the defenses that keep them from managing their problem situations.

4. Another important definition of confrontation relates to the skills of *resolving a conflict in close personal relationships.* This use of confrontation has a direct goal of building and maintaining close relationships. For example, friendships are built by establishing trust and expressing support and acceptance, but inevitably there are times when one or the other becomes angry because of a disagreement or destructive behaviors. If you are someone's friend, do you ignore conflicts or do you sit down and negotiate solutions that will benefit both? The first step in negotiation is to confront the opposition. A confrontation in this context is the direct expression of a person's cognitive and emotional view of the conflict while inviting the other person to do the same. It involves clarification and exploration of issues, the nature and strength of underlying needs of both parties, and current feelings about the conflict. Confrontation begins the process of problem solving which is basic to conflict resolution (Johnson, 1986). Again, this author stresses two cautions before this type of confrontation is undertaken. 1. There must be a high degree of relationship. In general, the stronger the relationship is between the two people, the more benefit will be de-

rived from the confrontation. 2. The emotional capacity of the person being confronted must be determined. For example, if the person's anxiety level is high or his or her motivation or ability to change is low, the confrontation should be put off since the confronter's main goal is to lead to an invitation for self-confrontation and self-examination in the other person. It is a mistake to assume that one should always confront a friend in order to resolve a conflict. It is a matter of prudent decision on the nature of the problem, the context, and the ability of the other to receive it (p. 222). Again, confrontation is a way of expressing concern, empathy and sympathy for a person, and a wish to increase involvement in the relationship.

5. Working with groups is part of the professional life of the chaplain. While this area is broad in scope, a few comments will be made regarding confrontation and groups. In a book by Stech and Ratliffe (1977), *Working in Groups: A Communication Manual for Leaders and Participants in Task-Oriented Groups*, the authors suggest that interpersonal problems in groups should be confronted directly and openly. Terms like team building and organization development reflect techniques used for group members to deal with their interpersonal relationships through direct discussion. Direct statements may be useful, such as: "I get the strong impression that we have a problem in this group. I think some of us are getting mad, and we need to deal with these feelings." The authors are quick to point out that the members must be willing to participate in this open confrontation (p. 132). Other authors, Hansen, Warner and Smith (1980), suggest that constructive con-

frontation in groups gives members an honest and immediate experience by allowing them to become aware of their impact on other persons. It can also indicate the measure of respect for their capacity to learn and make choices.

∽

Confrontation—Guidelines for Chaplains

1. A caring and trusting relationship has to be the foundation when confrontation is used in helping situations. In fact, it should be used when there is a willingness to maintain or increase involvement in or commitment to the relationship. "Hit-and-run" type of confrontations do more harm than good. This is the type of confrontation where the chaplain gives his or her views of, and feelings about, a sensitive issue and then disappears before the other person can respond. This tactic tends to escalate a lack of trust in the person and builds resentments and anger.

2. Confrontation can help to motivate a person to examine his or her reality in terms of motives, perceptions and behaviors if it is descriptive. It should be concise and specific. The most difficult issues for a person to face are the discrepancies and distortions in his or her own behavior. When confronting these issues, the chaplain must communicate openly and honestly his or her perceptions of, and feelings about, the issues involved.

Judgmental and interpretative statements may only threaten the person, so confrontations should be descriptive in nature. For example, a supervising chaplain may want to say to a trainee: "Frank, your twenty minute coffee breaks have been averaging three quarters of an hour. I find myself thinking dark thoughts about you. If you need more time on your breaks, I'd like you to keep a written record of it and make it up on another break." Here the confrontation is assertive and descriptive and in terms of specific behaviors. Frank knows exactly what the problem is and has a way of changing his behavior. If the confrontation is vague, it leaves the trainee with many questions and creates a new set of issues.

3. One of the chief goals for the use of confrontation is to help the person achieve the skill of self-examination. The chaplain confronts the behavior of the person in order to bring about some change of perspective about the issue. This change will not last over the long range if the person does not learn the skill of self-examination. This skill gives the person the responsibility to continue personal confrontations of the behavior when he or she is not in the therapy situation.

4. The timing of confrontations is an art in the helping process. Confrontation should be offered at a time when the person can best appreciate and use it. If it is not, the person may view the confrontation as an attack or as a potential reason for the rupture of the relationships. Remember that individuals in crisis are vulnerable, anxious, and attentive to potential threats to their safety and security. They come to the chaplain because they expect a trusting relationship, one where prudence and wisdom will predominate. For example, while the chaplain may know that the person's relationship with a woman outside his marriage is destructive, prudence will dictate that an immediate confrontation, no matter how cautiously it is done, will do more harm than good. Most often, the person has the insight already but needs a listening ear to help with the decision. There is no limit to the benefits of listening.

5. Vagueness in responses can be viewed by the person as a form of withholding information or playing the role of "top dog." As was stressed above, confrontations should be concise and specific. A vague and general confrontation such as "You are too demanding" may cause the person to be uncertain about your message and your attitude. Chaplains must remember that they are perceived in many different roles depending on the needs of the person: teacher, preacher, spiritual guide, minister, counselor, etc. Each of these roles holds a potential benefit for healing. If the person perceives the chaplain as a spiritual guide, and, at the same time, playing a "top dog" role in the relationship, he or she will be hesitant to share and self-disclose the real self. For this reason, confrontations should be clear, specific and concise so that there is little room for misinterpretation.

6. Chaplains should avoid the use of confrontation as a steady diet in their helping process. A sign of the inexperienced helper is the attitude that "Once I have the person listening and on the ropes, I should continue to confront until there is understanding." Ordinarily a person can hear one confrontation at a time. One extended confrontation, session after session, can become a punishing technique for the person. It may also be a sign that the chaplain may be dealing with his or her own issues. As mentioned above, confrontations should be accurately timed. Some therapists, like alcohol and drug counselors, use confrontation more frequently. Even in this case, it is recommended that a strong relationship of caring be developed with the person.

7. **A good sign that a confrontation has been effective is when the person is willing to examine his or her behavior with an eye toward change.** Usually the chaplain will see less denial and confusion in the person who has begun to accept the reality and meaning of the confrontation.

8. **Confrontations may help the person to re-examine the meaning found in strongly held attitudes and beliefs.** Many times people who find it difficult to recognize the effects of their attitudes and beliefs on others may find confrontations to be caring opportunities to examine the deeper meaning of their behavior. The effective confrontation opens up new avenues of insight and beliefs about the self. Confrontations are ineffective when they cause a person to close up and withdraw from searching for meaning. Here again, timing and empathic listening are most important. A chaplain should not confront unless there is a willingness to develop a deeper and more meaningful relationship with the person.

9. **Confrontations are meant to support the person.** For many, confrontation is viewed as an aggressive and assaultive behavior. In fact, the true nature of confrontation, as seen in the definitions above, is based in caring, empathy and support. The person can be brought into contact with his or her strengths and positive attributes in the process of a confrontation. In fact, this is exactly the outcome a person who confronts is seeking to bring to life in another. For example, a chaplain may say to a person who has remained abstinent from alcohol, "You were so nervous, but you didn't drink and get drunk or get into a fight this time. You can continue this behavior and feel in the future as good as you do right now." Another chaplain may say, "You say that your faith is not strong but you continually come to me in order to deepen your spiritual life. You must believe at some level." Here the past supports the attitude of the person while confronting the person to grow. Again, the chaplain intends to support the person's strengths.

10. **Confrontation may help a person to identify deeply held values and beliefs that may have been forgotten or denied.** A confrontation may bring to life the values that are at the foundation of a person's life, values which sustain meaning in the person. Sometimes guilt feelings, which may be quite appropriate, arise, causing some pain and remorse in the person. These feelings can be dealt with in the supportive and caring atmosphere of therapy.

These are only a few of the guidelines that can be expressed about this important technique in helping.

What is stressed over and over is the caring, genuine, honest, and supportive context in which confrontation must be practiced. Egan (1986) rightly calls confrontation a skill of challenge in the context of advanced accurate empathy.

∞

Confrontation: An Honest Experience in the Helping Relationship

Carkhuff and Berenson (1977) are well known for their research in the field of counseling. Referring to confrontation in counseling and life, they say, "What applies in an honest helping effort applies in life. What applies in life among growing and honest people applies in helping" (p. 296). They have found from their research at least two basic assumptions that helpers must be aware of before they attempt to help others. 1. At the highest levels, full honesty in counseling requires helpers who are fully committed to personal growth at any cost. Full honesty, except with those who are too fragile, sets the stage for greater self-definition. 2. Many helpers are less than they could be because they lack the minimal levels of understanding, genuineness, respect, and love. Some have been victimized and are the products of much more subtle starvation. At times these helper-victims excuse their inability to act constructively by postulating that each person protects a core within that should not be shared with others. As a consequence, the researchers found that helpers sometimes protect others from the core of themselves by passing on to others their (helpers') own fears. This leads to poor use of confrontation within an honest experience of helping.

Qualifications of Those Who Are Entitled
To Confront

Carkhuff and Berenson (1977) offer counselors four qualifications for those who in their estimation are entitled to confront others. A close inspection of these qualifications suggests that they apply to chaplains and all pastoral care and counseling helpers in a special way.

1. "Only those who demonstrate deep levels of understanding that go far beyond what is being said are potential sources of nourishment and may be entitled to confront." They suggest that confrontations based on deep levels of understanding result in better communication. Any confrontation without understanding results more often in inaccurate communication and can be destructive to the person confronted. In fact, confrontation that is based in understanding is the basis for deeper trust and respect. In our pastoral work, the development of trust, respect, and understanding is of primary importance since it is so characteristic of the spiritual message (p. 198).

2. "Only those who demonstrate deep and appropriate changing levels of regard and affect are potential sources of nourishment and may be entitled to confront." They are suggesting that the helper is in a mutual relationship with the helpee and that the helper is affected by the helpee in terms of respect and affect. Unchanging levels of regard and affect communicate to the helpee that he or she cannot have an impact on the helper. It also suggests that there is no real relationship but merely a "top-dog, under-dog" relationship (p. 199).

3. "Only those who are physically robust and live fully form a high level of energy are potential sources of nourishment and may be entitled to confront." The chaplain as helper must be willing to follow through

with the impact of constructive confrontations. This demands immense energy and durability on the part of the chaplain. At times confrontations open up a lengthy encounter and may result in feelings of abandonment for the person if dropped prematurely—just another in a long series of broken promises for the person in turmoil (p. 200).

4. "Only those who love what they respect and respect those whom they love are potential sources of nourishment and may be entitled to confront." The researchers suggest that the helper who has ceased to grow does not challenge the helpee to grow. They confront us as chaplains and pastoral counselors by saying that "love without respect is license to abuse." In truth, only the chaplains who are committed to growth in themselves recognize the struggle in others and experience the joy of their renewal (pp. 200–201).

Conclusion

In this article, the skill of confrontation has been presented as an important way of speaking the truth within an understanding relationship. The goal is to enhance the other's self-definition through a process of on-going self-examination and self-confrontation. Various definitions have been presented as well as ten guidelines for the use of confrontation.

Finally, to sum up the important issues raised in this article, the following definition is offered. Confrontation is a *caring, honest,* and *trusting* experience involving two or more *mutually responsible* individuals wherein a person seeking assistance comes face to face with his or her own *reality.* In this experience, the person is challenged to accept the *consequences of his or her behavior.* Confrontation exposes the chaplain and the person seeking assistance to *new information (self-knowledge, self-definition)* and offers the person a new *insight into the meaning* of the information in the context of the person's life experience. In this caring experience, the person is *challenged to change* his or her behavior, and, in the process, to *choose life.*

Suggested Readings

Carkhuff, R.R. and Berenson, B.G. (1977). *Beyond Counseling and Therapy.* New York: Holt, Rinehart and Winston.

Clinebell, H. (1984). *Basic Types of Pastoral Care and Counseling: Resources for the Ministry of Healing and Growth.* Nashville: Abingdon.

Cormier, W.H. and Cormier, L.S. (1979). *Interviewing Strategies for Helpers: A Guide to Assessment, Treatment, and Evaluation.* Nashville: Abingdon.

Daniels, V. and Horowitz, L.J. (1984). *Being and Caring: A Psychology for Living.* Palo Alto: Mayfield.

Egan, G. (1986). *The Skilled Helper: A Systematic Approach to Effective Helping.* California: Brooks/Cole.

Eisenberg, S. and Patterson, L.E. (1979). *Helping Clients with Special Concerns.* Chicago: Rand-McNally.

Hansen, J.C., Warner, R.W. and Smith, E.J. (1980). *Group Counseling: Theory and Process.* Chicago: Rand-McNally.

Johnson, D. (1986). *Reaching Out: Interpersonal Effectiveness and Self-Actualization.* New Jersey: Prentice-Hall.

Johnson, D. and Johnson, F.P. (1975). *Joining Together: Group Theory and Group Skills.* New Jersey: Prentice-Hall.

Miller, W.R. and Jackson, K.A. (1985). *Practical Psychology for Pastors.* New Jersey: Prentice-Hall.

Oates, W.E. (1974). *Pastoral Counseling.* Philadelphia: Westminster Press.

Osipow, S.H., Walsh, W.B. and Tosi, D.J. (1980). *A Survey of Counseling Methods.* Illinois: Dorsey Press.

Stech, E. and Ratliffe, S.A. (1977). *Working in Groups: A Communication Manual for Leaders and Participants in Task-Oriented Groups.* Illinois: National Textbook.

8

Anxiety: A Personal Discernment

Ann O'Shea

∾

During the 1990s it seems that Shakespeare's question "To be or not to be?" has become "To cope or not to cope?" A high level of stress and anxiety has impregnated our society. Transition, insecurities, fears, and losses surround us. Families are not stable, government is ineffective, work is unsure, and generally life is being threatened by feelings of anxiety.

In preparing to write this chapter on anxiety, I asked myself if the above picture was simply an Irish woman's view of reality, or if this was a universal perception of the 1990s. Research, readings, and years of ministry have convinced me that this is, indeed, a picture of today's society.

What makes this age so skeptical? The tentacles of change have uprooted structures, religious values, and the "status quo" of our lives. The unspoken imperative of "being in control of our lives" is being challenged. In essence the myth of "total control" is being destroyed by our iconoclastic world.

Within the parameters of this chapter, I invite the reader to examine anxiety, to assess the positive and negative aspects of anxiety, and to reflect on anxiety as a tool that could be used to facilitate balance in our lives.

ᗪᗷ

1. The Nature of Anxiety Is Universal

The desire to make decisions and affect outcomes, that is, to exercise control, is a basic feature of human behavior (White, 1959). This fundamental function, decision-making, establishes anxiety as a universal component of our lives. Saying "yes" to something means saying "no" to something else. Examining our choices uncovers our value system and reveals the anxiety that choice and change can surface.

Since the act of choosing is a core component of human nature, anxiety becomes a universal feeling. However, understanding of basic personality types indicates that some people are more prone to stress. For example a type A personality tends to be competitive, to function with a sense of urgency, to be aggressive, to need control over his or her environment (Pomerleau, Rodin, 1988). Although some personalities are more susceptible than others, all of us know that anxiety can impact on everything from our immune system to our closest relationships (Lerner, 1989).

Fear and anxiety, although related, are distinctly different. Rollo May, in his book, *The Meaning of Anxiety*, regards anxiety as "a response to threat on the basic level of the personality" and fear as "a response to threats before they get to this basic level."

When fear is the primary feeling, a person's attention is directed principally toward the person, the object, or the situation regarded as "dangerous" to one's well-being. Anxiety, in contrast, is a reaction to the apprehension of a threat that is vague, one that produces a feeling of diffusion, uncertainty and helplessness in the face of unspecified danger (Gill, 1985).

From this definition, it would be safe to say that ambiguity is the child of anxiety. Confusion and uncertainty highlight the presence of anxiety. When threats and fears paralyze our coping mechanisms, anxiety has become abnormal. Objectivity is lost in subjectivity, and the self is engulfed in "tunnel vision," which involves the inner psyche in conflict and turmoil.

2. Abnormal Anxiety Captures the Spirit

Most pastoral counselors and psychiatrists align anxiety with neurosis. They regard anxiety as a symptom exhibited by an individual who has a feeling of apprehension or uneasiness, usually with no clear cause (Gill, 1985).

The major anxiety disorders classified in the *Diagnostic and Statistical Manual* (DMS) of the American Psychiatric Association are as follows:

- Agoraphobia—the fear of being alone or in public places.
- Social phobia—the fear of public scrutiny, or of being humiliated.
- Panic disorder—recurring panic attacks without an appropriate stimulus.
- General anxiety disorder—a persistent state of anxiety without panic attacks in the absence of other diagnosis.
- Obsessive-compulsive disorder—anxiety associated with recurrent thoughts that the person recognizes as foreign, and, thus, resists.
- Situational anxiety—a state of anxiety related solely to a recent situational event.

- Post-traumatic stress disorder—a traumatic event or experience which is outside the range of usual human experience (i.e. earthquakes, accidents, etc.).

Even though we are all susceptible to the above listed disorders, most of us experience a more normal type of anxiety which can usually be tempered by reason. Anxiety becomes abnormal when the fears and insecurities of an individual seem to capture his or her spirit. In this instance, reason cannot temper doubt, and doubt cannot dialogue with fact. One's view of life is locked in an inner-perspective which is isolating and alienating.

3. Anxiety Is Triggered by Loss of Control

Trauma, change, transition, illness, and death are events which raise the levels of anxiety. When these circumstances occur, choice is not initial in these circumstances. Reaction, rather than response, is our first impulse. When control is shattered, anxiety is produced. Many times this type of anxiety expresses itself in anger, depression, or passivity.

4. Symptoms of Anxiety

There are a variety of thoughts and feelings which signify that anxiety is present. These include:

- Sudden feelings of dread or apprehension.
- Physical reactions, such as sweating palms, shaking, dizziness, loss of sleep, feelings of nausea.

- Excessive use of defense mechanisms.
- Patterns of avoidance and distancing.
- Feelings of panic which paralyze or cause over-reactions.
- Excessive work patterns.
- Fear of being perceived as out of control.
- Perfectionistic tendencies.
- Excessive fear of failure.

5. Anxiety, Whether Acute or Chronic, Affects Our Capacity To Be Healthy

While these may seem extreme, milder forms of the above symptoms may be present for years without the patient being aware of the anxiety. Low levels of anxiety can have equally devastating long-term effects. Prolonged states of anxiety can produce a chemical imbalance within our bodies or any number of psychosomatic illnesses which need medical attention.

6. Anxiety Affects Relationships

Dealing with our individual anxieties is necessary if we want to be able to deal compassionately with others. "Only through our connectedness to others can we really know and enhance the self, and only through working on the self can we begin to enhance our connectedness to others" (Lerner, 1989). Thus, care for ourselves parallels our care for others. This parallel process validates the ancient proverb that says "we cannot do for others what we cannot do for ourselves." Whether ministering to our own anxieties, or to others who are anxious, it is good to remember that anxiety permeates relationships, keeping intimacy from occurring.

7. Relief Is Possible and Available

While anxiety is a part of everyday life, the condition does not necessarily have to debilitate us. There are many ways to reduce the symptoms of anxiety. Consulting a physician is necessary when physical symptoms indicate that stress is affecting our health. While there are medications which assist in the reduction of anxiety, behavior and attitudinal adjustments are far more efficacious in reducing anxiety long-term. Some methods which have proven successful for others are:

- Learning to temper our sense of responsibility can assist us in setting limits on our feelings of apprehension.
- Relaxation techniques can provide relief from anxiety.
- Prayer and meditation can replace anxiety as a means of coping with control.
- Communication, rather than isolation or withdrawal, can assist in tempering anxiety.
- Cognitive restructuring will assist in learning how to process and deal with anxiety.
- Deep breathing creates a natural less anxious state.

8. Anxiety Has Both Positive and Negative Aspects

Since anxiety is a powerful emotion, it does have the power to mobilize or to paralyze us. It also has the potential to increase our creativity, as well as to decrease our energy levels. James J. Gill, S.J., M.D., states: "If there is any single affect that qualifies as one of the best blessings, and also one of the worst scourges in human existence, it is anxiety" (*Clinical Handbook of Pastoral Counseling,* 1985).

The tension which this multi-faceted emotion produces can stimulate heroic rescues, as well as prevent a person from speaking in public. Other constructive functions of anxiety are pointed out by O. Hobort Mower in *Learning Theory and Personality Dynamics.* In this text, Mower affirms anxiety "as a sign that human nature is trying to heal itself and make itself whole, just as it can be understood as a signal that an individual is experiencing threat and thus suffering" (Mower, 1945).

Anxiety surfaces when our basic values/personalities are threatened. From this threat, changes and choices which confront our ethical/moral values facilitate our professional, personal, and spiritual growth. Naming and reclaiming our values in the face of stress and conflict allows us to discover our authentic identity. Learning to live with our strengths and weaknesses frees us to experience the paradoxical potential of our human nature. In essence, attending to our anxieties can lead to integration instead of disintegration. Anxiety, in its positive mode, can be the emotion which helps us to balance idealism with realism, limitations with strengths, and apprehension with trust.

9. Balance Is an Antidote for Anxiety

When asked to write this chapter, I had to temper my anxiety with realistic parameters. My desire to share had to be balanced with my apprehension. I had to reflect on my perception of anxiety, read and research to broaden my perspective, and then strive to express an objective presentation which could be influenced by my subjective view. Perspectives, it seems to me, define our realities. Being human implies that we have limitations.

Accepting our limitations can bring balance to our perfectionistic tendencies. Self-perceptions directly influence our ability to manage ambiguities and apprehen-
sions. Further, our religious traditions influence and are
influenced by our perceptions. With this in mind, I
would like to illustrate how my Christian heritage
enriches my view of managing anxiety. In this faith tradition, we believe that Jesus is the Mediator, as well as
the Savior, of humanity. The God-Man entered life, and,
like all prophets, became a voice crying in the wilderness
of his society. Jesus' feelings of anxiety and fear are documented in the gospel. The synoptic writers of the New
Testament tell us that Jesus wept, that he agonized in
the garden, and that he uttered such words as "My heart
is nearly broken with sorrow" (Mt 26:38).

10. Jesus Managed Anxiety

How did Jesus live with his anxieties? By claiming
and advocating trust, he preached such things as: "Everything is possible to a person who trusts" (Mk 9:23).
"Which of you by worrying can add a moment to his
life-span? If the smallest things are beyond power, why
be anxious about the rest?" (Lk 12:25–26). "Stop worrying—seek God's kingship over you and all else will follow" (Lk 12:32). "Do not live in fear, little flock"
(Lk 12:29).

As a Christian, my perception of humanity is rooted
in the message of Christianity. I view trust as a paradoxical element which links me with my creator. Trust enables me to perceive relating as the primary function
which gives meaning to life. Trust empowers and en-

ables us to transform isolation into feelings of connectedness. For me, peace is trust in action. Long ago my religious tradition freed me from the myth of valuing total control as a basis for inner security. Today's society, like all other societies, gets stuck in panic and fear when security and control become the predominant perspective which defines happiness. Thus, from my faith tradition, I offer trust as a key to temper anxiety and I propose that the art of balancing life's values can be anxiety's gift to us. If used properly, anxiety can be a tool which facilitates our ability to cope, as well as our ability to create.

∽

Suggested Readings

Gill, J. (1984). "Anxiety and Stress," in Wicks, R.J., Parsons, R.D. and Capps, D.E. (eds.), *Clinical Handbook of Pastoral Counseling.* New York: Paulist Press.

Lerner, G. (1989). *The Dance of Intimacy.* New York: Harper & Row.

May, R. (1977). *The Meaning of Anxiety* (rev. ed.). New York: W.W. Norton and Co., Inc.

Mower, O.H. and Ullman, A.D. (1945). "Time as a Determinant in Integrative Learning," *Psychology Review*, 52:2.

Pomerleau, O.F. and Rodin, J. (1988). "Behavioral Medicine and Health Psychology," in Bergen, A. and

Garfield, S.L., *Handbook of Psychotherapy and Behavioral Change*. New York: John Wiley & Sons.

White, R.W. (1959). "Motivation Reconsidered: The Concept of Competence," in *Psychological Review*, quoting Adler, *Science of Living*. New York: Greenburgh Co.

9

Crisis Intervention

Beverly Elaine Eanes, R.N., Ph.D.

∾

The Oriental symbol for crisis means both danger and opportunity. Though this may be a time of great difficulty for the person in crisis, if handled in a timely manner with caring as well as expertise, it may lead to the client's renewed growth and personal development.

It is the immediacy of the current problem, the disequilibrium of psychological balance which must first be addressed. Only later, when there is some approximation of pre-crisis functioning, is one able to delve into underlying psychological problems. It is a decisive matter of prioritizing or triage.

Caplan (1964) sees crisis as self-limiting, approximately four to six weeks. It is during this crucial time that the appropriate helper can have the maximum effect. The client is in a very vulnerable state and is psychologically ready for guidance and support. It is your presence—really being there with your continued support—that is the essential first step.

Crises do overwhelm the patient and family but they do not need to overwhelm the chaplain. Below are ten things to remember when dealing with crises.

∼

1. Be There

The vulnerable person appears lost and is probably in emotional shock, physical shock or both. The
boundaries which are normally attributed to their life
have disappeared, and they are floundering to grasp
something on which to find a rational hold. You as a
chaplain represent strength, both in the power
beyond earthly wisdom, and in the tangible presence
of your caring.

The importance of your supportive presence cannot
be overemphasized, for you act as a bridge toward the
restoration of the person's equilibrium. Your crisis intervention must, of necessity, be time-limited. Therefore, the initial strength of your real presence serves as a
bond to concentrate the efforts of brief therapy toward
the therapeutic goals.

2. Crises Can Produce Positive Growth

Crisis, unlike the more negative view of stress, can
have positive growth-promoting potential. Energy must
be mobilized, so that what may at first be viewed as a
loss or a threat to equilibrium may eventually become a
challenge. Therefore, it is essential to be really present
to the person in crisis, to hear, see, and feel what is being
communicated. Though this communication may be
personally indicative of this client's specific crisis, it
may also be similar in pattern to others in crisis. It is
important to understand these patterns, while at the
same time keeping the individual's circumstances and
needs in mind.

3. There Are Four Types of Crises

A crisis is a disruption in the person's equilibrium, and his or her usual coping mechanisms do not prove adequate to restore that equilibrium. There are four types of crises: maturational, situational, intrapsychic, and existential.

a. *Maturational:* developmental crises which occur as the person moves through the stages of life—attempting to make the transitions from child, adolescent, adult, and later life. Typical maturational crises are independent living, marriage, having a child, and retirement.

b. *Situational:* traumas such as the loss of a loved one through death or divorce, job loss or failure in business or school. Cavanagh (1982) speaks of the two other types of traumas which can precipitate a crisis.

c. *Intrapsychic:* traumas which are "internal events that create great anxiety." These include: identity confusion; needing to leave a relationship or job for the sake of one's sanity; profound questioning of one's faith, or homosexual feelings emerging.

d. *Existential:* recognizing the loss of meaning in one's life—a sudden emptiness of purpose such as in relationships or in a job.

4. Stages of Crisis

There are five stages of crisis according to Golan (1978): hazardous event, vulnerable state, precipitating factor, active crisis state and reintegration.

The hazardous event is a stressful circumstance that disturbs an individual's equilibrium and initiates a series of actions and reactions. The event may be unanticipated as in the death of a family member or an anticipated life transition such as parenthood.

The vulnerable state occurs when the hazardous event is subjectively interpreted, usually as a threat, loss or challenge (Rapoport, 1965). The individual attempts to reduce the resulting increased tension by one or more of the person's usual coping mechanisms. If these coping mechanisms are unsuccessful, there is increased tension, with the eventual consequence that the person becomes unable to function in an effective manner.

The precipitating factor may be like the "last straw," an event that converts this now vulnerable state into a crisis state. The person becomes a new parent, but the baby is born very prematurely, adding tremendously to the stress of this life transition. In other situations, the hazardous event and the precipitating factor may be identical.

The active crisis state is disequilibrium with the following phases: psychological and physical agitation, preoccupation with events which led to the crisis, and later returning gradually to a state of equilibrium. Usually during this state the person will seek help because he or she recognizes the inadequacy of the usual coping mechanisms.

Reintegration or restoration of equilibrium is dependent on the individual's ability to objectively evaluate the crisis situation and to develop and utilize effective coping strategies.

5. Assessment: Patient's Problem, Condition, and Coping Mechanisms

The situation must first be defined clearly in order to facilitate more specific solutions. Good observational skills are necessary at this point while simultaneously asking pertinent questions. Aguilera (1990) suggests observations "to determine his level of anxiety, expressive movements, emotional tone, verbal responses, and attitudinal changes." Important questions to consider are *why* the individual is coming *now* for help, and *what* makes *today different.* The focus is on the immediate problem, and is usually something that happened within the last ten days to two weeks.

Aguilera next looks at what meaning the event has for the person and whether or not his perception is accurate or distorted.

This situation is then related to any previously similar situations and how the individual handled them. Have any of these coping mechanisms been tried this time and with what result? What other possibilities are there and how would the results be projected? Visualization and guided imagery can be helpful here.

One of the most important assessments seen by Aguilera is to determine if the person is homicidal or suicidal. Questions which need to be asked include: Does he have a specific plan, and is it beyond just the thinking stage? How lethal is the plan and how feasible is it? If there is an imminent threat, then a psychiatric evaluation with hospitalization may be necessary.

6. Support Systems

The patient's support system must be assessed and includes not only personal supports such as friends and relatives, but also religion, community educational programs, self-help groups, and social service agencies.

The close friend, relative, or caring co-worker can assist the chaplain by being available to the patient by phone or in person. Remember to ask or assess if the support person is actually helpful to the patient or is part of an unhealthy alliance. When the relationship is unhealthy, it may exacerbate the patient's stress. Or the nature of the trauma itself may cause the support person to abandon the patient as in the case of financial loss, disfigurement, or rape.

When a chaplain is providing pastoral care, and not pastoral counseling, then the patient should be referred to a counselor/therapist for short or long term counseling as needed. When a patient is socially isolated, the counselor's support is especially necessary.

Resources in the community such as education for parenting, support groups for substance abusers, and agencies which can facilitate aid (financial, medical, etc.) can give further support.

7. Planning the Intervention

The type of intervention is determined by a number of factors including: the type of crisis, the patient's resources/support system, and the skills/theoretical orientation of the chaplain. The techniques most commonly used are: cognitive, affective, behavioral, and environmental (agency referral). Eventually the patient needs to understand not only the situation (or developmental phase) precipitating the crisis, but also his or her own participation in the crisis. When the timing is right, insight occurs, facilitating growth and possible prevention of future problems.

But, for the immediate crisis resolution, the intervention must be goal directed. There must be a concentrated commitment of both the chaplain and patient. The chaplain is an active participant with a directive role focusing on the here and now.

The chaplain and patient need to brainstorm, to

pool their resources and weigh what will work best in the situation. This helps the patient to see the problem from a different vantage point and to call forth coping skills perhaps forgotten, or to learn new skills. The added support of the chaplain and others facilitates risking these older and newer coping skills. It is vital that the patient be instrumental in devising his own plan of action. This will help him to get beyond feeling inadequate in the face of the crisis.

8. Intervention

Some of the following techniques (Aguilera, 1990) are useful and a basic guideline for crisis intervention.

• Helping the individual to cognitively understand his particular crisis. This may need to be a direct approach as the patient often "sees no relationship between a hazardous situation occurring in life and extreme discomfort of disequilibrium that he is experiencing" (Morley et al., 1967).

• Helping the individual bring into the open his present feelings which he may not be able to access. Frequently feelings such as anger, grief or guilt may have been suppressed. Helping the patient recognize and express these feelings will go a long way toward the immediate reduction of tension (Morley et al., 1967).

• Helping the individual to behaviorally work through the coping process. Small concrete steps may be taken in the way of assignments which would seem to be feasible. Once one step is accomplished, the patient will have a greater belief in his adequacy to try the next step.

• Finally, the patient can call upon his or her environmental support system to aid in getting through the crisis.

9. Crisis Resolution

As the person begins to move forward toward equilibrium, he or she will be able to leave the pastoral care process at least as far as crisis intervention is concerned. Now is the time, in the last sessions, to evaluate how the patient has adapted to this trauma. Which coping mechanisms have worked, and which have not? The object was not to create drastic behavioral changes but to reduce symptoms of disequilibrium and to try to restore the person to at least the pre-crisis level of functioning. The progress that the patient has made is summarized.

The decision to terminate is a joint one between the chaplain and the patient. Because the person may be still somewhat vulnerable, the need for a support outside of counseling is even more vital now that the crisis counseling is terminating. The chaplain may let the patient know that he or she may return for assistance in the future should the need arise. However, do not hesitate to refer the patient for counseling if the crisis seems to uncover unresolved issues. In addition, some chaplains may make a follow-up call to the patient to see how he or she is doing, which allows the counselor to evaluate the progress that has been made and to determine if referral is necessary.

10. Future Planning

The crisis intervention will have helped the patient in developing new coping strategies which may be used in the future. Throughout the crisis intervention, the chaplain has been supportive, but at the same time should have promoted as much self-reliance on the part of the patient as possible. Therefore, the patient is much more able to independently adapt to future traumas.

This is a significant step in promoting the patient's mental health.

∽

Suggested Readings

Aguilera, Donna C. (1990). *Crisis Intervention: Theory and Methodology.* St. Louis: The C.V. Mosby Company.

Caplan, G. (1964). *Principles of Preventive Psychiatry.* New York: Basic Books, Inc.

Cavanagh, Michael E. (1982). *The Counseling Experience: A Theoretical and Practical Approach.* Prospect Heights: Waveland Press.

Golan, Naomi (1978). *Treatment in Crisis Situations.* New York: Free Press.

Morley, W.E., Messick, J.M., and Aguilera, D.C. (1967). "Paradigms of Intervention," *Journal of Psychiatric Nursing,* 5:537.

Rapoport, Lydia (1965). "The State of Crisis: Some Theoretical Considerations," in *Crisis Intervention: Selected Readings,* ed. by Howard J. Parad. New York: Family Service Association of America.

10

When the Patient Is a Woman

Anne Ross Stewart, M.R.E., M.Div., D.Min.

∽

Regardless of our sex, most of us want a chaplain or pastoral care person to have some of the following qualities—to be:

1. an empathic listener, who responds accurately and appropriately to our feelings and condition;

2. a person willing to take the time to be with us, yet who is sensitive to our limitations and need for rest;

3. a person who is willing to acknowledge and express concern for our friends and family, especially while we are hospitalized or confined to home;

4. a person who has a sense of hope, but who is not afraid to be with those whose hope is fading or gone, as well as those who maintain good morale in spite of pain and suffering.

In selecting ten specific issues that a chaplain needs to know in working with women patients, the first topic to be addressed will be that of some of the common cultural differences between men and women. In addition to these socially influenced values that women often hold, five problems common to many women will be discussed. These include women who are depressed, women who suffer with PMS (pre-menstrual syndrome), women who have menopausal difficulty, women who have been sexually assaulted, and women who have been battered. These are some particular problems which are primarily women's issues because of female biology. When women are dealing with these issues, it is to their benefit and to their care-giver's credit if a deep awareness of the women's perspective is understood. Some medical problems which women experience are related to their sense of sexual self-esteem, and affect their perceptions of themselves as women, lovers, wives, and/or mothers. For purposes of illustration, we will also discuss four situations that deal specifically with biological problems that women may encounter. Those considered will be breast cancer, the problem of infertility, miscarriage and infant death, and hysterectomy. For many women, the chaplain or parish pastor may serve as the initial or an on-going supportive care-giver. In many of these instances some longer-term work will be necessary, and an appropriate referral to a pastoral counselor or other therapist may be in order. Sensitive issues requiring pastoral awareness will be highlighted for each of the situations presented.

∞

1. Common Cultural Differences

Some differences between men and women may be more culturally based than biologically determined. Rather than make the claim that all men are a certain way and all women a certain other way, the following chart is offered as a way of summarizing some of the generalizations that often are true about the ways North American men and women are different. The chart was

developed by Memrie McKay based on her reading of
Carol Gilligan's *In a Different Voice* (1982). When a
chaplain is listening to a female patient discuss her situation, he or she may be helped by seeing if the values
reflected tend to be similar to those more frequently emphasized by women.

Females	Males
primary concern—rela-tionships and caring	*primary concern*—hier-archy of rights and rules
task of connection (responsible attachment)	task of separation (individuation)
ambiguity of both/and	absolutes of either/or
morality of self-abnegation	morality of self-development
ethic of care:	*ethic of justice:*
premise—non-violence no one should be hurt	premise—equality everyone should be treated the same
life focus: affiliation	*life focus:* achievement
persistent concern: exclusion	*persistent concern:* priorities
who is left out?	what or who goes first?
world view: network of relationships	*world view:* individual standing alone
world coherence: human connection	*world coherence:* system of rules.

2. Depression

   Because some degree of depression accompanies
many cases of hospitalization regardless of the cause of

hospitalization, some comments about why depression is such a common problem for women may prove helpful here. Unless the chaplain's setting happens to be a mental hospital, the depressions that the chaplain frequently encounters in female patients will not likely be those that are characterized as psychiatric disorders. It may be useful for the chaplain to know the differences between dysthymia or depressive neurosis, major depression, and the bipolar depressions of cyclothymia and bipolar disorder, when a patient is "clinically" depressed as well as dealing with another illness (DSM-III-R, 1987). In these cases the chaplain may want the patient's permission to consult with another therapist to see what support may be offered. In many cases, however, even though a patient's moderate depression may not merit a psychiatric label, it is a natural area of focus for the chaplain.

It is noteworthy to point out that more women than men are diagnosed with depressive illnesses. Depression begins earlier in life for females, and women have more depressive episodes and longer episodes than men do. Both depressive and manic-depressive psychoses have genetic components. Some researchers propose that some manic-depressive psychoses may be sex-linked, and related to female hormones (Hoyenga & Hoyenga, 1979). One study of women who had recently given birth found that sixty-seven percent of them had experienced crying spells in the first ten days after giving birth, and that twenty-eight percent of them cried for at least one hour or more. Post-partum depression seems to occur more frequently after the first or second birth, and in women who have had a history of menstrual difficulty. Women differ in their sensitivity to hormonal imbalance, and this can be due to genetic inheritance as well as environmental and cultural stress (Hoyenga & Hoyenga).

Christie Neuger notes the disparity in statistics regarding the occurrence of depression in women, but women are more depressed than men at a minimum ratio of 2 to 1, although some studies suggest six times as many women as men are depressed. If we take the lower estimate, "we are talking about as many as 26 million women who struggle with feelings of depression at some point in their lives; more than one out of four women experience at least mild depression" (Neuger, in Glaz and Moessner, 1991, p. 147). Abuse, economics, education, low self-esteem, and sexist theological beliefs can all contribute to women's depression. When the chaplain encounters a depressed woman it helps to recognize that psychological and social factors, as well as patriarchal theologies, may be partially responsible.

Miriam Greenspan also speaks of a general kind of depression found in many women which she attributes to the repressed anger women naturally have in realizing their second-class status in a sexist, patriarchal culture. Sexism is still a reality, and in many fields women are still receiving less pay for identical education and experience. In a number of surveys, including one by Greenspan, she found that depression is still the number one problem that brings women to therapy (Greenspan, 1983). Greenspan also points out that the fact that women are the majority of patients in all sectors of the psychiatric system except for state and county mental hospitals is not due to the fact that women are sicker than men, but that they more readily present themselves for treatment; and their "illnesses" are often "the systematically socially produced symptoms of sexual inequality" (p. 7). She speaks of the difficulty of distinguishing ordinary depression from clinical depression, pointing out that most of us from time to time experience some feelings of dejection, helplessness, fatigue, hopelessness, self-hatred, and emptiness. And some of us periodically have changes in appetite, weight, sleeping patterns, and some of the other symptoms of depression. While not ruling out the psychiatric reality of clinical depression, Greenspan does show how "the major ingredients of depression—the feelings of hopelessness, helplessness, worthlessness, futility, and suppressed rage—are the affective components of the objective social condition of female powerlessness in male society" (p. 193).

The hospital chaplain will often find that the depression experienced by female patients is of a generalized nature. Since most patients are likely to experience a sense of powerlessness over the condition that has led to their hospitalization, and since dealing with any kind of physical ailment is likely to be somewhat depressing, a woman who is hospitalized may be adding layers of depression to some pre-existing feelings of depression. The chaplain can be empathic with the woman's plight, and also be encouraging of any efforts that she may make to empower herself. Because depression may be the result of long-term internalization of oppression, it may take a therapeutic journey to release the stored up anger as an empowering force. Therefore, if the chaplain finds the patient significantly depressed, an appropriate referral for a consultation to evaluate the need for therapy and/or medication may be in order. In the meantime, frequent supportive visits by the chaplain should not be seen as "merely adjunctive"; they are essential. The depression experienced by women patients may be related to some specific kinds of losses, such as the loss of a breast, a baby, a uterus, as well as some related loss of self-esteem as a woman. Some of these losses will be noted in subsequent items in this chapter.

3. Premenstrual Syndrome (PMS) and Menopause

Two phenomena related to a woman's reproductive cycle that have achieved prominence in the past two decades are that of PMS (Premenstrual Syndrome) and menopause. The subject of many articles in popular women's magazines, these experiences have also become subjects for more serious scientific research, and apparently, because of poor methodologies, much more research is needed for more conclusive understandings. Besides the need for treatment of uncomfortable physical symptoms there has been a need to understand and treat the emotional distress that has been associated with PMS and menopause. While the hospital chaplain will not likely see patients who are admitted with PMS or menopause as the condition for treatment, many of their patients may suffer from symptoms ascribed to these conditions in addition to whatever their primary presenting illness may be. Therefore, what are some things that the care-giver needs to know? What are some known facts, and what remains to be seen about these conditions?

One definition of PMS is "the presence of any symptoms or complaints that regularly come just before or during early menstruation, but are absent at other times of the cycle" (Dalton, 1990, p. 21). Common complaints include somatic symptoms (fluid retention, abdominal bloating, back and abdominal cramps, breast tenderness) and mood fluctuations (irritability, anxiety, depression, anger). In spite of the similarity of these complaints among many women, there is not yet conclusive evidence from research about what causes the complaints. Before more is said about that, however, it is important to note that women do want their symptoms and complaints to be heard and to be taken seriously, even if the cause is still uncertain. Some contemporary feminists are particularly concerned that a false accusation of hormonal imbalance may be too simplistic and only perpetuate sexist attitudes that because of their hormones, women are not reliable or competent workers.

K.E. Paige's research indicated that a woman's religious beliefs were influential in how she experienced her menstrual cycle. Among Jewish women with certain religious taboos and Catholic women who held a traditional view that a woman's place is in the home, there were more severe physical and emotional symptoms associated with menstruation. The debate is raging about whether a social psychological theory of menstrual symptoms is more accurate than theories which are based on hormonal cause (Archer & Lloyd, 1985). No one hypothesis adequately explains the group of symptoms associated with PMS. Anne Fausto-Sterling (1985) says, in short, "PMS is a disease in search of a definition and a cause" (p. 100).

While research continues, many women still experience moderate and severe physical discomfort as well as fluctuations in mood. The pastoral care-giver needs to accept the reality of a patient's distress. She needs to be taken seriously, and wants empathy, understanding, and acceptance. If she feels angry or depressed or irritable, she needs permission to express these feelings, not judgment for having them. Some women may be helped by meditation or relaxation techniques. Cullen and

Dean (in Glaz & Moessner, 1991, pp. 88–89) suggest that as care-givers "can accept and integrate the idea of rhythmicity and the creative cycles of menstruation, we can find innovative ways to help women appreciate the link between the 'letting go' of menstrual fluid and the spiritual 'letting go' so necessary for spiritual oneness and release of energy." Self-help groups also seem to be effective in helping women deal with PMS. "Among the functions outlined are mutual support, promotion of understanding regarding menstrual problems, dispelling myths, and development of personal strategies for coping with pain (e.g. massage, exercise, relaxation)" (Fielding and Bosanko in Broome and Wallace, 1984, p. 234).

Menopause refers to the final menstrual period "and occurs during the climacteric. The climacteric is that phase in the aging process of women marking the transition from the reproductive stage of life to the non-reproductive stage" (Fausto-Sterling, p. 114). While those technical distinctions have been made by the scientific community, common usage of the word menopause seems to fit the definition of climacteric, which indicates a phase of life, rather than the specific event of the last period. Some researchers suggest that the period of the climacteric, the long-term physiological process caused by the involution of the ovaries, may last as long as twenty years, beginning ten years before menopause and lasting ten years after menopause. Therefore, while menopause technically means the cessation of menstruation, when most people think of women going through "the change of life" and the event of menopause, they really are referring to the climacteric process. That process may vary from a number of months to a number of years.

There are several agreed upon physical changes that occur to most women following menopause. Hot flashes and vaginal dryness are fairly common, and many women find relief from these symptoms by ERT, estrogen replacement therapy. For many women a combination of estrogen and progesterone seems to offer the best combination of results. Estrogen does not cease with menopause, but there is a gradual lowering in ovarian estrogen. Osteoporosis, a brittleness of the bone which can be so severe that it can cripple older women, also seems to develop after estrogen levels have declined, but there are other factors that may contribute to osteoporosis, such as "sedentary life styles, genetic predisposition, hormonal imbalance, vitamin deficiencies, high-protein diets, and cigarette smoking" (Fausto-Sterling, p. 118).

More debate exists about the emotional consequences of menopause. Hormonal changes occurring due to menopause have been held responsible for a wide range of symptoms, including fatigue, irritability, insomnia, headaches, depression, and anxiety. Although it is likely that many post-menopausal women might have some of these symptoms, to link them explicitly with the climacteric may be too much a generalization. Anne Fausto-Sterling (1985) notes that contemporary studies show no specific correlation between menopause and depression. She cites a survey by the Boston Women's Health Collective of more than two hundred menopausal or post-menopausal women, in which "about two-third of them felt either positively or neutrally about a variety of changes they had undergone, while a whopping 90 percent felt okay or happy about the loss of childbearing ability" (p. 120).

Dean and Cullen (1991) have noted that there are

many "real life" issues that occur for women about the age of fifty which may be the primary struggles that some women are dealing with. Because these women may also be menopausal, menopause may be falsely identified as the main culprit. At this time during the life cycle, women may be dealing with the empty nest, struggle over career, marital stress, illness and death of parents, disappointments of past and present, as well as fear of the future. Depression that has sometimes been attributed to menopause may be more accurately attributed to some of these life events. Certainly, if a woman's primary life focus has been on childbearing and raising a family, she may experience more depression if she is unable to refocus a sense of purpose. Pastoral care-givers need to understand the particular life history of each woman at this time in order to grasp the existential meaning of menopause for her. If the loss of generativity is a major issue, the chaplain may be able to help her claim the biological loss, but also to see some hope in new ways of contributing to the human community that are not related to the reproductive role. Feelings of ambivalence about menopause are quite normal. "Women express both regret and hope, nostalgia and current reality, loss and gain, pride and disappointment, a longing and a relief as they try to deal with a life period that each person must negotiate" (p. 91). Chaplains need to guard against any condescending or trivializing attitudes toward menopause, be open to what women are needing to express about their feelings about this time in their life cycle, help women link with other women who have similar issues, and be encouraging of educational opportunities that can provide accurate information as well as a supportive environment for discussing these real life issues.

4. Sexual Assault

If a chaplain is available for emergency room crises it is likely that women who have been sexually assaulted may welcome some pastoral care. Rape victims have some particular needs that the chaplain should know about. To best serve these women, chaplains as well as other pastoral care providers need to do some special reading about rape and rape victims, and the books mentioned in the footnotes are a few examples of useful resources. In addition, workshops provided by crisis centers may be of immense help to a novice in this area. In many counties and cities there are services provided for rape victims, and these treatment centers often provide educational opportunities as well as informative brochures.

Rape has the legal definition of "carnal knowledge of a person by force and against that person's will. Two elements are necessary to constitute rape: 1) sexual intercourse and 2) commission of the act forcibly and without consent" (Hilberman, 1976, p. xi). Women coming to a hospital as a result of a sexual assault are usually emergency patients. They may come alone, or they may be accompanied by a friend, a police officer, and/or a counselor or volunteer from a sexual assault service. The first thing a chaplain needs to ascertain is whether the patient wants the chaplain's services at all, and, if so, if medical treatment is needed immediately, or if the chaplain's reassurance is needed first to enable the victim to calm down enough in order to receive medical attention. When the patient needs medical treatment first, she should be reassured that she will be able to receive pastoral care as soon as her medical needs are addressed.

A medical examination following a sexual assault will likely include most of the following components: 1) If there are cuts or injuries, first aid will be administered, and follow-up care may be required. 2) A blood test and vaginal fluid smear test will be taken to see if there is any evidence of a venereal disease or a pregnancy prior to the rape. 3) Antibiotic drugs may be given to prevent any disease from passing from the assailant to the woman. Follow-up testing is needed to determine if an attack has resulted in a pregnancy or a venereal disease. 4) Sometimes medications are offered which may prevent a pregnancy that could occur from the attack. Women need to be encouraged to understand the pros and cons of taking these medications before making a decision (Montgomery County, n.d.).

Follow-up treatment typically has some of these components: Two weeks after the assault the patient has a smear test to check for certain sexually transmitted diseases (STDs), including gonorrhea and chlamydia. Six weeks after the assault, a blood test is needed to check for other STDs, including syphilis and hepatitis, and exposure to the AIDS virus. If a regular menstrual period is missed, two weeks later a urine or blood test should be given to determine if there is a pregnancy. Finally, until all of these test have been administered, the woman is advised to practice only protected sex—e.g. using condoms during sexual activity.

In addition to being aware of the common medical procedures done while in the hospital and upon discharge, the chaplain also needs to have some understanding of the role of the police officer who may be present during the emergency room procedures. Because rape is a criminal offense, evidence must be collected and documented so that the victim will be able to make a strong case if she chooses to prosecute. A female police officer will be present during the medical examination if the assault is reported to the police. The doctor will make notes and collect evidence to show force and/or penetration. Color photographs may be taken as evidence. Vaginal, anal, and/or oral fluid samples may be taken, depending on the type of assault. Clothing and underwear will be collected and bagged. Pulled head and pubic hairs may also be needed. Saliva and blood samples are also typical, and sometimes fingernails may be clipped or scraped to collect any assailant tissue or blood. In addition to the collection of all of this data, the police officer will also need to get a complete description of the attack.

Rape is a crisis situation, and the rape victim has experienced a shocking, traumatic event. Because the victim has often felt that her life has been threatened as well as feeling a complete loss of control, she is likely to feel quite distraught and overwhelmed. The rapist may have been a complete stranger, a date, or a spouse. Although the emotional reaction will vary, there are some feelings that are very common. Initial responses to the rape may range from crying and raging to an apparent calmness that may be more of a state of shock or feeling "numb." Other feelings include a sense of helplessness, anxiety, humiliation, guilt, fear, embarrassment, self-blame, anger, and revenge.

If the chaplain on duty is male, he may need to make a referral to a female colleague. Following a sexual assault a woman may have extreme difficulty relating to any male in an authority role, whether police, medical doctor, chaplain, pastor, or counselor, especially if the professional is a stranger to her. Male chaplains need to avoid patronizing or protective reactions, and also should be cautious about touching the victim. Any move that might be perceived as physically or sexually threatening will likely alarm the patient. Because women do not generally appreciate specific questions about the actual rape, the chaplain should avoid probing questions about the details of the rape, and should concentrate on how the woman feels now and what bothers her most. Her lifestyle has been disrupted in five areas: physical, emotional, social, sexual, and spiritual.

Marie Fortune's *Sexual Violence: The Unmentionable Sin* (1983) is an excellent resource for chaplains to study. One chapter focuses on the religious concerns and pastoral issues to be addressed. Some of the main points of this chapter are noted here. First, the experience of rape presents a further crisis for the victim. Victims ask questions like, "Why is this happening to me?" "Why did God allow this to happen?" "Am I being punished for some sin I have committed?" Victims need compassion, support, and comfort. As important as theological questions may be, the chaplain needs to be careful not to pay so much attention to the intellectual challenge of the meaning of evil and suffering that the pain of the particular victim is overlooked. In the days and weeks following a sexual assault, a woman will likely try to make sense out of the experience. Because rape leaves a woman feeling so out of control, she will try to understand the circumstances surrounding the rape experience and do everything she can to avoid similar circumstances in the future.

Some of the feelings that a victim may begin to express to a hospital chaplain will take a long time to work through. Most assault victims will need follow-up counseling, and the chaplain can play a helpful role by providing some referral information to the woman. Questions about the meaning of suffering, feelings of guilt, shame, and anger, and feelings of abandonment by God are themes frequently heard by pastoral counselors who work with rape victims. The hospital chaplain can prepare the way for subsequent therapy by validating the woman's feelings and issues, and encouraging her to obtain further therapeutic help. The chaplain can help her understand that this experience will not only impact her personally, but that her family, husband, boyfriend, or friends may have a difficult time coping with their feelings about the rape. She needs to hear that victims and their significant others can react to this crisis in a variety of ways, and that there isn't one right way to move through and beyond the rape experience.

5. The Battered Woman

Another kind of problem the chaplain may encounter among woman patients, especially if assigned to emergency room coverage, is the victim of spouse abuse, popularly known as the battered wife. A National Crime Survey reported that 2.1 million women were victims of physical abuse by their partners at least once during a twelve-month period. Thirty-two percent of these women were abused at least a second time. It is estimated that every fifteen seconds a woman is battered. Thirty percent of female homicide victims are killed by their husbands or boyfriends. "The U.S. Surgeon General's Report states that physical battering is the single largest cause of injury to women in the United States; it surpasses muggings, rapes, and automobile accidents combined" (Garma in Glaz and Moessner, 1191, p. 129). Since 1982 over a million women each year seek medical treatment for injuries sustained in battering incidents, and twenty percent require emergency medical care.

Many women who seek emergency medical treatment are too embarrassed and ashamed to reveal the true source of their injuries. They can still benefit from the pastoral care of a chaplain even if they are not ready to disclose the abuse. Many are willing and needing to share the trauma. Some of the counselor characteristics that a battered woman will find helpful, as suggested by Anne Horton (Horton & Williamson, 1988) include: (1) being sensitive and empathetic, (2) ability to listen, respect, and validate, rather than minimize or discredit, (3) offering practical, specific suggestions, not platitudes—educate and inform rather than preach, challenge, or blame. Other skills are listed, but may be more applicable to the pastor or counselor who provides ongoing support after the woman leaves the hospital.

Chaplains, as well as other pastoral care-givers, need to be aware of their own value systems and religious beliefs to see if they may interfere with their ability to minister to the victim of spousal abuse. Since scripture has often been misused to justify abuse, a chaplain needs to be prepared to contradict this notion. The physical safety of the victim is the first and primary concern. She may need to be encouraged to leave her spouse for a time until safety needs are met, and then she can decide what she wants to do about the marital relationship. Obviously counseling is indicated for the couple, and it may require months of work. If a woman is ready to leave an abusive relationship permanently, she needs to be supported in that decision. The woman needs to be listened to carefully, allowing her own story to unfold at her own pace. In spite of feelings of hopelessness and helplessness, some reassurance that it is possible to re-establish control over her life is helpful. She needs to know that millions of women have struggled with this painful situation and have worked their way through the crisis. She needs to know that no matter how imperfect she is, violent behavior toward her is neither appropriate nor deserved.

The chaplain's role with the battered spouse will likely be very limited, but can be extremely valuable. In addition to providing immediate support and comfort, the chaplain can be immensely helpful in providing referral information. Local crisis centers and shelters may be available to the patient. One excellent resource for pastoral care providers is The National Coalition Against Domestic Violence (P.O. Box 15127, Washington, DC 20003-0127). The battered woman needs education as well as support in coping with her situation. If she is a member of a faith community, she will need to decide if she wants to inform her pastor of her need for support. If possible, the chaplain might provide the woman with a copy of Marie Fortune's *Keeping the Faith: Questions and Answers for the Abused Woman.* Other books that the chaplain will find helpful include Rita-Lou Clarke's *Pastoral Care of Battered Women* and Carol Bingham's *Doorway to Response: The Role of Clergy in Ministry with Battered Women.*

6. Breast Cancer

Because breast cancer is second only to lung cancer in women and will affect one out of nine women in their lifetimes, it is important for the pastoral care-giver to have some understanding of the emotional impact that this disease has on women. There are a variety of kinds of breast cancers with different prognoses due to different growth rates and degrees of malignancy. The early detection of breast cancer has resulted in lowering the risk of death. Self-examination of the breast has resulted in women discovering ninety percent of breast lumps themselves. Probably most women who fear getting breast cancer have less of a fear of death, and a stronger fear of disfigurement and the loss of sexual attractiveness. Our culture has put a high value on the physical appearance of both sexes, and women have known since their early teens that their breasts are fascinating and appealing to most men. In fact, although the concept of penis envy is a familiar concept in the psychoanalytic literature, there is some acknowledgement that there is a corresponding breast and/or womb envy in men. How much the envy on the part of both men and women of the other's biological difference is debatable; the penis may be primarily symbolic of the power men have in society, while the breast and womb may represent the power that women have in reproduction, nurturing, and affiliation. Harriet Lerner (1988) notes that "society's intense idealization, devaluation, and literal obsession with breasts seems to point to the significance of such a phenomenon [breast envy]. . . . It is not my intention to popularize the notion of breast envy, but rather to suggest that male envy of female sex characteristics and reproductive capacity is a widespread and conspicuously ignored dynamic" (pp. 8–9).

In Jane Ussher's book *The Psychology of the Female Body* (1989), she notes that beginning in puberty and throughout adulthood, a woman's breasts are important symbols of her sexuality. She observes that both in the U.S. and Britain the amount of photography devoted to breasts reinforces their importance to female sexual identity. The paradox that the media approves of cleavage in a dinner dress, indicating that a certain amount of exposure is sexy, but that breastfeeding an infant in public is not socially acceptable, is indicative that the breasts are valued more for their erotic appeal to men than their functional role for feeding infants. "The promotion of these images of 'perfect' breasts makes the average woman feel imperfect, and makes her conceptualize her visible breasts—rather than her less visible vulva—as her main erogenous zone. This can result in the need for psycho-sexual counseling for women who have undergone breast surgery, and as a result of it see their sexual life as having ended" (p. 23).

The chaplain needs to understand that the disfigurement of the breast, even "lumpectomy," as well as a partial or full mastectomy of one or both breasts, is an emotional counterpart to male castration anxieties because the woman may fear she is no longer an acceptable sexual partner. Mary James Dean and Mary Louise Cullen (1991) note that if a woman has to lose a breast, her ability to cope will depend upon a variety of factors: "(1) support of family and friends, especially her spouse, (2) the point in the life cycle at which the breast is lost, (3) what the woman brings to the situation, that is, her psychosocial parameters and coping abilities, (4) the psychological management of the patient by the health care team, (5) what the breast means to the woman herself, and (6) the extent of the disease" (p. 97). Dean and Cullen suggest a number of important things for ministers to be attuned to. Most women go through a period of shock, denial, and anger when learning of breast cancer.

Their emotional needs are often not understood or dealt with adequately by the medical staff. Chaplains can support the patient's right "to full information, to multiple medical opinions, to access to a collaborative medical team, and to respectful treatment of the person" (p. 100).

It is important to encourage the woman with breast cancer to share her feelings of anger and loss with her spouse or significant others, and the chaplain may help in this process. It is also very useful for women with breast cancer to be encouraged to find support from other women who have had breast cancer. Reach for Recovery is a national supportive network for women with breast cancer. To be able to communicate her complex feelings is a primary need of the patient, and these feelings may be "of fear, loss, anger, and grief, along with the complex feelings that accompany mutilation of the body. Most women feel a sense of guilt or sin, that they are being punished in some way. All feel their own mortality and an anger and grieving over the loss and limitation imposed by the cancer. Spiritual caregivers must first be human with women in this crisis and be willing to share the grieving" (Dean and Cullen, p. 101).

Infertility, Miscarriage and Infant Death, and Hysterectomy

The topics of infertility, miscarriage and infant death, and hysterectomy have a common thread: they all deal with either the loss of a child or the loss of the potential of a biological child. For women who wish to bear children, this may be a profound loss. Even women who have given birth to one child may have deep sorrow if they cannot have another child. In today's American culture, women who do not marry or who do not bear children are not targets of social ostracism as they might have been in years past. For women who do want to marry and who do not find suitable partners, and for women who do want to bear children and cannot, their sense of personal loss may still be profound, even though society will not hold their situation against them.

Pastoral care-givers need to be aware that grief counseling is the general focus for much of their work with these women and/or their spouses. With most women who have experienced a miscarriage or an infant death, the possibility of another pregnancy still exists for many, but trying to present this hope prematurely without dealing with the grief of the present would be an insensitive error on the part of a ministering person. Likewise, alternative parenting that may be available for some who experience the events of infertility, miscarriage, infant death, or hysterectomy is not possible or desirable for everyone.

7. Infertility

Although some couples choose not to have children, infertility commonly refers to the involuntary state of being childless. Many couples who are unsuccessful in accomplishing a pregnancy go through extensive testing to determine the possible cause of infertility. In the United States recent statistics put twenty percent of the cause as undetermined, while the remaining eighty percent seems to be fairly equally divided between problems of the husband and those of the wife. Some research has been done to see to what extent infertility may be a psychosomatic disorder, but this is at best dubious. Michael Humphrey suggests that it may be best to view fertility as a biological variable which may be modi-

fied by social and emotional factors. Coming to terms
with infertility, however, is an ordeal for those who
strongly want to become parents (Humphrey in Broome
and Wallace, 1984).

Dean and Cullen assert that "the infertile woman
experiences many feelings about control, self-image,
self-esteem and sexuality. Responses to infertility are
usually surprise, denial, anger, depression (sadness, despair), guilt, and grief. Marital conflict often occurs, as
one spouse quickly blames the other" (p. 92). Anger in
the form of rage or depression is common. The pastoral
care-giver needs to be empathic to the power of these
feelings and may find theological themes in the psalms
of lament or the anguish of Job that are similar to the
grief and anger experienced by these women, as well as
women who miscarry, lose a baby in infancy, or have
their wombs removed.

8. Miscarriage

A miscarriage is the spontaneous abortion of a developing fetus or embryo. About seventy-five percent of
miscarriages occur during the first trimester of pregnancy, and many of these are caused by hormonal de-
fects. Most other miscarriages occur during the second
trimester and are due to hormonal imbalances or a weak
cervix. Some women miscarry without ever knowing
they are pregnant. Any miscarriage that occurs after the
second month is likely to be accompanied by heavy
bleeding, cramping, and some mild labor pains. Although most miscarriages are not dangerous to women,
the emotional consequences may be more devastating
(Francoeur, 1982). Grieving, anger and guilt are emotions frequently experienced. Not all miscarriages will

require hospitalization, but some will. Sometimes it will be the woman's pastor or rabbi who provides the pastoral care, but the hospital chaplain may be the first care-giver to know in many instances. Sometimes the chaplain may be the only religious figure to know because women and couples often have felt that their sense of loss over a miscarriage isn't important enough to take up their pastor's time. If a chaplain learns of a miscarriage, taking a pastoral initiative will often be helpful in allowing the woman or couple to express their feelings. Anger at God is common, and people are often reluctant to let a minister know about their hostile feelings toward God. A pastoral care-giver can be very helpful in letting the patient know that persons of faith can be very angry at God, and that God not only can understand their anger, but may indeed be suffering with them in their loss.

9. Infant Death

Certainly infant death evokes similar feelings. In this situation, the pregnancy has resulted in the birth of a baby, and there has been time to celebrate the baby's safe arrival. To then have to experience the baby's untimely death feels like a cruel joke. Shock, disbelief, anger, guilt, a profound sense of loss, depression, are common reactions. "The gift of time, and presence and shared agony is the best support during this life crisis" (Dean and Cullen, p. 96). Chaplains and other pastoral care-givers need to provide the ministry of a listening presence. Also, many women and families are helped by having a ritual that marks the significance of the loss. There are some rituals that have been written to help the pastoral care-giver in this situation. Again, people who go through this kind of loss can be greatly helped if a chaplain or pastor helps them to network with others who have experienced a similar loss. With divorce statistics approaching eighty-five percent for couples following the death of an infant, significant pastoral intervention might make the difference in saving the marriage, even though the baby is lost.

10. Hysterectomy

Having a hysterectomy before she has been able to have a child will be a very painful event for a woman who has wanted to give birth. For women who have given birth to at least one child, there still may be a significant sense of loss in not being able to have more children. Even if a woman has had several children, a hysterectomy can still be a time of mourning for many women because it does mark the end of the possibility of biologically being able to reproduce. Before a woman makes the decision to have a hysterectomy she needs to be encouraged to feel certain that it is a medical necessity, and not a hasty decision to "cure" certain menopausal symptoms. One scholar suggests that it has been far too easy for the medical profession to remove a woman's womb without clear evidence that there is a strong need for this radical surgery (Ussher, p. 114).

How a woman responds emotionally to a hysterectomy will depend on several factors. If childbearing has been an important part of her identity as a woman or if she perceives her uterus to be the essence of her sexual identity, a hysterectomy may put her in an emotional crisis. Obviously, if she has never had a child or wanted more children, the loss of her reproductive capability will be traumatic. On the other hand, women who see themselves as nurturers and care-givers and know that a loss of a reproductive organ will not necessarily mean a loss of that important role will have less trouble accepting a hysterectomy. Women who are clear they do not want more children, and women who are experiencing considerable physical discomfort or who know of a cancerous condition, may be quite relieved to have a hysterectomy behind them. Once again, the pastoral care-giver must be sensitive to the particular situation of this patient to see what kind of support she needs. In all cases, the pastoral care-giver should be supportive in helping her to obtain the information she needs to understand the reason for surgery and the probable outcomes of the surgery. What the operation means for a particular woman's feminine identity will vary considerably. An open atmosphere to explore feelings and raise questions of meaning is important.

∞

Conclusion

In this chapter we have focused on some particular issues that a chaplain needs to know about in order to provide effective ministry when the patient is a woman. Obviously, in choosing only ten issues, this is a representative but not an exhaustive list of important items. In ministering to women patients the chaplain will be most helpful in remembering that there are complex factors influencing how a woman will react to her medical predicament. While many generalizations have been noted to alert the chaplain to probable responses in different situations, each woman remains a unique individual with her particular history. As in other ministerial situations, listening intently, and drawing out the woman's own experience and feelings, will be most helpful. Anticipating some of the likely reactions, the chaplain can be better prepared to provide immediate care, as well as equipped with knowledge to supply helpful referral information for follow-up care.

Suggested Readings

Archer, John and Lloyd, Barbara (1985). *Sex and Gender.* Cambridge: Cambridge University Press.

Bingham, Carol F., ed. (1986). *Doorway to Response: The Role of Clergy in Ministry with Battered Women.* Springfield: Interfaith Committee Against Domestic Violence.

Clarke, Rita-Lous (1986). *Pastoral Care of Battered Women.* Philadelphia: Westminster Press.

Cooke, David J. "A Psychosocial Study of the Climacteric," in Broome, Annabel and Wallace, Louise (1984). *Psychology and Gynaecological Problems.* London and New York: Tavistock Publications.

Dalton, Katharina (1990). *Once a Month: The Original Premenstrual Syndrome Handbook.* Claremont: Hunter House.

Dean, Mary James and Cullen, Mary Louise. "Women's Body: Spiritual Needs and Theological Presence," in Glaz, Maxine and Moessner, Jeanne (1991). *Women in Travail and Transition: A New Pastoral Care.* Minneapolis: Augsburg Fortress.

Fausto-Sterling, Anne (1985). *Myths of Gender: Biological Theories about Women and Men.* New York: Basic Books, Inc.

Fielding, Dorothy and Bosanko, Carole. "Psychological Aspects of the Menstruum and Premenstruum," in Broome, Annabel and Wallace, Louise (1984). *Psychology and Gynaecological Problems.* London and New York: Tavistock Publications.

Fortune, Marie (1987). *Keeping the Faith: Questions and Answers for the Abused Woman.* San Francisco: Harper & Row.

Francoeur, Robert (1982). *Becoming a Sexual Person.* New York: John Wiley & Sons.

Garma, JoAnn M. "A Cry of Anguish: The Battered Woman," in Glaz, Maxine and Moessner, Jeanne (1991). *Women in Travail and Transition: A New Pastoral Care.* Minneapolis: Augsburg Fortress.

Gilligan, Carol (1982). *In a Different Voice.* Massachusetts: Harvard University Press.

Greenspan, Miriam (1983). *A New Approach to Women and Therapy.* New York: McGraw-Hill Book Company.

Hilderman, Elaine (1976). *The Rape Victim.* Washington, DC: American Psychiatric Association.

Hoff, Lee Ann (1990). *Battered Women as Survivors.* New York: Routledge.

Horton, Anne L. and Williamson, Judith A. (1988). *Abuse and Religion: When Praying Isn't Enough.* Lexington: D.C. Heath and Company.

Hoyenga, Katharine Blick and Hoyenga, Kermit T. (1979). *The Question of Sex Differences.* Boston: Little, Brown and Company.

Humphrey, Michael. "Infertility and Alternative Parenting," in Broome, Annabel and Wallace, Louise (1984). *Psychology and Gynaecological Problems.* London and New York: Tavistock Publications.

Lerner, Harriet (1988). *Women in Therapy.* Northvale: Jason Aronson, Inc.

McKay, Memrie (1986). Unpublished Master's Thesis, Loyola College in Maryland.

Montgomery County Government, Department of Addiction, Victim and Mental Health Services (no date). *After Sexual Assault: A Comprehensive Guide.* Rockville, MD.

Neuger, Christie Cozad. "Women's Depression: Lives at Risk," in Glaz, Maxine and Moessner, Jeanne Stevenson (1992). *Women in Travail & Transition: A New Pastoral Care.* Minneapolis: Augsburg Fortress.

Pellauer, Mary and Chester, Barbara and Boyajian, Jane, editors (1987). *Sexual Assault and Abuse: A Handbook for Clergy and Religious Professionals.* San Francisco: Harper & Row.

Ruether, Rosemary Radford (1986). *Women-Church: Theology and Practice of Feminist Liturgical Communities.* New York: Harper & Row.

Tannen, Deborah (1990). *You Just Don't Understand: Women and Men in Conversation.* New York: William Morrow and Company.

Ussher, Jane M. (1989). *The Psychology of the Female Body.* London and New York: Routledge.

Notes on the Contributors

Sharon E. Cheston, Ed.D. is Associate Professor and Associate Chair of the Pastoral Counseling Department, Loyola College in Maryland, In addition to her full-time faculty assignent, she has taught at St. Mary's University and Seminary as a visiting faculty member.

Dr. Cheston's publications include *Making Effective Referrals*, a Behavioral Science Book Service Selection of the Month, and *Mary, Mother of All: Protestant Perspectives and Experiences of Medjugorje*. Chapters in other books and journal articles include topics on sexual abuse, supervision, and short-term therapy.

Dr. Cheston has been involved with the education and supervision of counselors since 1976 and is sought after as a lecturer, workshop leader and consultant to churches and non-profit organizations. Focusing on therapy to professional helpers, she maintains a limited practice in the suburbs of Baltimore.

⌇

Robert J. Wicks, Psy.D. is Professor and Director of Program Development for Pastoral Counseling at Loyola College in Maryland, and recently also served on the visiting faculty of both Princeton Theological Seminary and Washington Theological Union. Dr. Wicks, who is a graduate of Hahnemann Medical College as well as Fairfield and St. John's Universities, has also taught in universities and in professional schools of psychology, medicine, social work, theology and nursing.

In addition, he has directed mental health treatment programs in the United States and the Orient.

Dr. Wicks has published a number of books. He is the senior Co-Editor of the two volumes of *Clinical Handbook of Pastoral Counseling*, is author of the widely read books *Availability: The Problem and the Gift*, *Living Simply in an Anxious World*, and *Seeking Perspective*. His latest book is entitled *Touching the Holy*.

Dr. Wicks also maintains a private practice in Maryland, is Book Review Editor for the National Association of Catholic Chaplains, is General Editor of *Integration Books: Studies in Pastoral Psychology, Theology, and Spirituality*, published by Paulist Press, and is a member of both the Editorial Board of *Human Development* and the Editorial Committee of the *Journal of Pastoral Care*. His major areas of expertise include the integration of psychology, spirituality, and pastoral counseling.

∽

Anthony J. DeConciliis, C.S.C., D.Min. is a priest in the Congregation of the Holy Cross, Eastern Province. He has been involved in higher education as a faculty member, administrator and campus minister at the University of Portland, King's College and Bridgewater State College, respectively. He is a faculty member in the Department of Psychology at Stonehill College.

∽

Beverly Elaine Eanes, R.N., Ph.D. is Director of M.S. and C.A.S. Clinical Education in Pastoral Counseling at Loyola College. Formerly on the faculties of Georgetown University, Columbia Union College, and the Johns Hopkins Hospital, she has been involved in health care for more than thirty years. She is a member of the American Nurses Association, American Counseling Association and the American Association of Pastoral Counselors. Dr. Eanes has been a Chaplain Associate and is a Nationally Certified Counselor and a Clinical Specialist in Psychiatric and Mental Health Nursing. She received her B.S.N. from Johns Hopkins University, her M.S. and M.Ed. from the University of Maryland, and her Ph.D. in Pastoral Counseling from Loyola College.

∾

Edward R. Killackey, M.M. has been a missioner for 35 years, in ordained ministry. Most recently he is an M.S. graduate of Loyola College in Maryland. He now engages himself in health care ministry to the chronologically-gifted.

∾

Anthony F. Krisak, S.S., S.T.D. is a priest of the Diocese of Trenton and a member of the Society of St. Sulpice. He currently serves as Assistant Professor of Pastoral Counseling and Theological Consultant at Loyola

College in Maryland. He is author of *Liturgical Commentary: The Order of Christian Funerals* (FDLC, 1989).

∽

Ann O'Shea has a B.A. in Humanities from Gwynedd Mercy College and an M.A. in Religious Education from LaSalle University. She has Certification as a Full Supervisor from the National Association of Catholic Chaplains. Her professional experience has allowed her to establish and direct departments of Pastoral Care and Clinical Pastoral Education Programs, as well as to Chair the United States Catholic Conference Commission on Certification.

In the past she has organized and participated in seminars and lectures for Ministry Training, published articles in N.A.C.C. publications and the *Journal of Pastoral Supervision.*

Presently, she is Director of Mission Effectiveness at St. Agnes Medical Center in South Philadelphia, and a member of the Franciscan Health System of Aston, Pennsylvania C.P.E. Advisory Board.

∽

Duane F. Reinert, O.F.M. Cap., holds a Ph.D. in Pastoral Counseling from Loyola College in Maryland. Currently he is campus minister at Haskell Indian Junior College, Lawrence, Kansas, and is on the staff of the Psychological Service Center at Conception Seminary College, Conception, Missouri.

∽

William J. Sneck, S.J., Ph.D. is an Associate Professor of Pastoral Counseling at Loyola College in Maryland and a licensed psychologist. His chapter grew out of giving workshops around the U.S. on the "hard" emotions of hurt, anger, fear, guilt and shame.

∽

Ann Ross Stewart, M.R.E., M.Div., D.Min. is a United Methodist clergywoman who received the three degrees listed from Wesley Theological Seminary. A native of Maryland, she currently serves as Director of the Gaithersburg Pastoral Counseling Center, an ecumenical agency, and is an adjunct faculty member of Loyola College's Department of Pastoral Counseling. A member of AASECT, clinical member of AAMFT, CPC in Maryland, she is a Fellow in AAPC, and currently is chairperson of the Atlantic Region of AAPC.